LOOK AT YOURSELF

LOOK AT YOURSELF

JOHN SHERMAN

LOOK AT YOURSELF

Book & Cover Design: Carla Sherman
Photo: Robert Wang

Edited by Carla Sherman

This book contains the edited transcriptions of the meetings during the 2007 Retreat with John Sherman in Ojai, California on November 2 through 6, 2007.

SilentHeart Press/RiverGanga Foundation
PO Box 1566
Ojai, California 93024 USA
Phone: +1 (805) 649-1600
http://www.johnsherman.org
http://www.riverganga.org
http://www.silentheart.net
info@riverganga.org

Published in the United States of America
ISBN   0-9718246-7-3
ISBN-13 978-0-9718246-7-6

To Gangaji.

Acknowledgments

We thank all of the wonderful people who participated in these dialogues, and our dear friends who provided the financial means for the publication of this book.

Our sincere gratitude to Carla Cripps, who patiently transcribed the recordings of these meetings, to Paul Robinson and Andre Best, who proofread the text, and to Julian and Judie Plowden for their invaluable comments and suggestions.

To look at yourself just once, and then again, and then again... is to move from the endless work of self-definition to the endless adventure of self-discovery.

Look At Yourself

Contents

Look At Yourself

Meeting 1

November 2, 2007 - Evening

Here we are. I want to welcome you to this retreat. I want to tell you how grateful I am that you are here. My understanding is that we have quite a diverse group here. We have people who have been with us for a long time, perhaps many years, and we have people who have never been in a meeting with us before, all gathered together for these five days, these next eight or nine meetings, in a circumstance that is pretty intense and focused. I can't wait to see how it turns out. I am happy you are here, I am grateful for your presence here. I am grateful for your attention and your willingness to listen and to argue with me.

So far as I can tell, from everything I have seen, and heard, most lives are given over to trying to make the life better. This is to be expected. After all, we didn't ask to be here, we just kind of dropped in, and we find ourselves in this combination fun/horror house of craziness and madness, filled with stories about what we are and what we should be, what we should want, what we should not want, what we should do to go about getting those things, what we should do to go about not getting those things. Most of our life is given over to trying to sort through these competing and complementary forces that impinge on us all the time — the body's sensations, the thoughts, the understandings, the memories, the regrets, the yearnings. And we don't know what to do about them.

Most of us, at some point, go to church, pray to god, and ask for god's help. We try to understand god, try to understand religion, and try to understand our place in the scheme of things. Maybe we become spiritual. Maybe the more intent we are and the more open we are to see what is happening to us, the more likely we are to happen upon the idea that there is a spiritual solution, the idea that there is something different and more profound than religion.

So, here we are. Now we may think that we have made a great leap out of our old ways as a result of happening upon the spiritual solution, but in fact, we are doing the same old thing — we are trying to fix our lives, trying to make them better, trying to make them satisfactory, sweeter and clearer.

The reason I say all this is because this time when we are here together is not for that. We are not here to fix our lives. By all means, fix your life if you can, and if you must. But this time we are together here is not for that. The reason I want to make that clear is because what I have to offer, and what I am going to be wrestling with you about, and talking to you about, and laughing with you about, and joking with you about throughout this time has nothing to do with that. It is not like a development of the path that you have been following; it is not a development in your spiritual life. It is not like that. It is not the next step on your path, "Once I was a Christian, and then I was a Hare Krishna, and then I was a Buddhist, and then I really had it together! But then I found this other thing…" It is not like that.

What I am here to speak with you about has absolutely nothing to do with any of that; it doesn't have anything to do with fixing your life, it doesn't have anything to do with making your thoughts clean, it doesn't have anything to do with ridding you of bad desire and helping you fan the flames of good desire. It doesn't have anything to do with understanding reality, and it doesn't have anything to do with understanding the actual, absolute reality of things. It doesn't have anything to do with understanding anything at all. Well, a little bit, maybe, just enough to get started. Because what I have seen is that pretty much all I can do, if I can do anything worthwhile at all, is to get you started. I can't give you what I want you to see. I can't describe for you the reality that I am inviting you to witness for yourself. I can't do any of that. I can't even tell you by what particular method you are to embark upon this investigation that I am going to be speaking about. I mean, really, I have got nothing. But I can get you started.

And if I get you started, that should be enough. Nothing we are going to be discussing here has anything to do with anything you have read, done, practiced, understood, or not understood. It has nothing to do with anything spiritual, and nothing to do with anything religious. It has nothing to do with anything but the truth. That is all I am interested in: the truth.

Not the truth that I can then proclaim to you, such as "All is one." Well, that is not exactly true, but true enough. Or "There is nothing but love." Well, that is true enough, but it leaves out so much. So, the point of this looking for the truth has nothing to do with finding some way to describe the truth. The truth has been described to death for six thousand years now. We don't need to do that here.

So, what is the point? Here is the point: it is all about *identity*. It really is. And it is not surprising that the media, the advertising, and the whole way in which the popular culture presents itself is all about identity. It is all about being what you want to be, and not being what they want you to be, and being all you can be, and you know, "What am I?" and "That's not who I am..." All, in a kind of ignorant, unconscious way, honoring of the fact that it is all about identity. It really is, it is all about identity. I used to not want to say that, because I used to have a much greater desire to be nuanced and subtle. But that has kind of fallen away. It is all about identity, and here is what I mean by that.

There is a thread that has run through all of the attempts that we have made for thousands of years to get something real about our life. And that thread is the insight that we are not what we believe ourselves to be. That's why it is all about identity. We are not what we believe ourselves to be. There is a false belief operating within our consciousness by means of which we unconsciously believe, without the need to defend, or discuss, or consider, or reflect upon it, that we are our lives — our mind, our thoughts, our history, our memory, our expectations, the things we have done that are good, the things we have done that are bad, and what we have learned from them, what we need now, what is going to be good for us, what is going to be bad for us — the whole totality of our lives. There is nothing to us but these lives. And because there is nothing to us but these lives, there is a belief that rests at the bottom of consciousness that "I am this life." That belief that I am this life gives rise within me to an endless upwelling of fearfulness and anxiety — that I'll think the wrong thing, that I'll miss it, that I'll forget what I'm supposed to be, that I will do the wrong thing, that I'll want the wrong thing, that I'll make a mistake, that somebody else won't see me as I see myself.

This fear and anxiety that is endlessly upwelling within us, driving all of our efforts and all of our activities, is based upon this belief that I am this life, and that I am at stake here, and that by god, I'd better not think the wrong thing, and I'd better not make the wrong spiritual choice, and I'd better not pretend I understand, but I'd better not admit that I don't understand, either. I am this life, I am at stake here, this is all there is, just this, just this life.

If that is true, then we ought to know it for sure, rather than just assuming it and kind of dancing around it. If it is true that I am my life and nothing else, then I'm perfectly right to be trying to fix my life. I am doing exactly the right thing, and I'd better get better at it, because life is slipping away. If it is true I am my life, then I'd want to know, once and for all, whether all this religious gorgeousness and all of this spiritual seduction are false and a waste of my time.

It turns out that this belief is a lie. But you can't know that because I tell you. This belief is absolutely hidden from your consciousness. It is not something that you see, and then say, "Okay, I'm going to do away with that!" It is the lens through which we see everything. But it's not true, it really isn't. And this is not new, either. This is old stuff, this is what the gurus, the teachers, the practitioners and the avatars have been telling us from the very beginning, "You are not what you think you are, and that's the problem."

Some of them have told us how we can fix this problem: you can become something different, you can transform your mind, and you can transcend the pettiness and the smallness of your life. You can do this practice and get these experiences of peace, and these onrushing experiences of clarity and satisfaction. You can do these practices for the next ten lifetimes, hundred lifetimes, thousand lifetimes, and eventually obtain liberation, moksha, or freedom. And, so far as we can tell, the more we read about it, this freedom is the end of the mind: no thought, no life, no nothing. Just nothing.

For thousands of years, we have tried to rid ourselves of all false belief about what we are, about our relationship with god, about our relationship with each other, about the truth of things, the reality of things. We have tried to do this by reading, by listening to those who can speak about these things, by trying to understand, by studying, by meditating, by practicing, by trying to get a deeper understanding, a deeper conviction of what I am: I know what I am, I am Consciousness, I am Awareness, I am the Totality. And we try, and we try, and no matter how hard we try, here we are, still trying — six thousand years, seven thousand years of trying. A few, we are told, break out here and there, like sparks in a dark sky. A few, we are told, break free of the trap of human existence, and those few, we are told, have passed on to us the methods whereby we can follow them out of this trap.

But we have been following them for... how long? Six thousand years? Seven thousand years? And still, just a few, we are told, break loose, here and there. If it is true that we suffer from a false belief about what we are, then it should also, obviously, indisputably, be true that the only solution for that is the truth.

Not more preaching, not more understanding, not more states that come and go, not more samadhis, just the truth. If it is true that the only problem is a false belief about what we are, and it is this that infects and inflicts upon humanity all of the horror that humanity inflicts upon itself, then the only solution is the truth.

Here's the good news: the truth is really simple. It is not what we think. Really, it is not. The truth of our nature is here, always, no matter what else is going on, no matter what else is happening in your mind, in your life, in your hopes and dreams, in your past and your future, in your relationships or in your therapy. No matter what else is happening in your life, you are here, and it is all happening in you. Sleep comes and goes. Satisfaction comes and goes. Confusion comes and goes. Clarity comes and goes. Hatred comes and goes. Love comes and goes. You remain. You are never absent. How hard can it be?

If you undertake this investigation into the truth of what you are, what you are looking for is just you. It's not something special, it's not something new, it's just you, exactly, precisely, only you. So how hard can that be? Whatever else is going on, no matter what else is happening in my mind or my body, it is absolutely possible for me to stop for just a second, and direct my attention inward and backwards. In any set of circumstances, there are two main things: there is the grab bag of circumstances playing, rising, falling, scuffling with thoughts and sensations, and so forth, and there is the *seer* of the circumstances. If you will look for the seer, that's looking backwards. If you will look for the seer, you will find the truth, which is not the seer.

How hard can that be? We can make it hard, right? We can get into all kinds of philosophical, metaphysical and spiritual disputes and contentions about the impossibility of anything seeing itself. If I see it, then it must be something other than me. So, it can't be me. How do I get around that particular little conundrum? Really, it is so much simpler than all of that. All that stuff is beside the point, just beside the point — not bad, or good, just beside the point. Just look for yourself. Look for the seer. Just decline for a moment to look at the seen, and look at the seer. Look for it.

Or, consider what I have said about the fact that you are always here, that you are never absent. You have never been absent, not for a heartbeat. Other things are present, then absent, present, absent... Some of them stay longer, some of them stay for a shorter time, but you are stuck with it all. You are never gone, you are never absent, you never get to take a break, you are always here. There is no place for you to go, because you are all there is, and you are always here.

Therefore, you are ordinary. You are absolutely ordinary. You are ordinary beyond all possible understanding of the word *ordinary*. You are what you see all the time. There is never a time when you are not. You are ordinary. You are here. You are never absent. You have never been changed. You have never been touched. You have never been hurt or helped by anything that happens in your life. You are the same.

How hard is it, then, to try to find something underneath, or between, or within, or above this whole phantasmagoria of display, circumstance, and phenomena? How hard is it to look between the cracks to find something that never moves, that is always the same? It is a cliché to say, "I am the same now as when I was three years old." It is a cliché to speak about looking in the mirror and seeing this old geezer and saying, "Whoa, what is this? That's not me! Who is that?" That is a cliché because it points to something that we know, which is that *we have never changed*. So, look for that. Look for something that is permanent. If you find something, and it was not here a minute ago and now it is here, you can be sure that in the next minute it will be gone again. It is not permanent. Look for what is permanent. Look for what doesn't change. Look for what is always here. Look for the seer, or look for what is permanent, or look for yourself, or look for what feels like you, that which feels like the certainty that you are.

You are, right? Can anybody actually dispute the fact that they exist? I mean, apart from spiritual mumbo-jumbo, you are here. You exist. You *are*. This is absolutely certain. In fact, it is the only thing that is absolutely certain. Everything else is conditional. One day it looks like this, next day it looks like that. What I liked yesterday, I don't like today. But the certainty that you exist is conditioned on nothing. Nothing gives rise to it except you, your presence. So look for that. Consider. Reflect. Ask yourself, Is there any doubt in my mind that I exist? What makes me so sure that I exist? Look and see.

Here's what I tell you, from my heart, from my own experience — having nothing to gain from telling you this other than to have you consider the possibility that there is some truth to it — that if you will, by whatever means necessary, whether it is by looking to see if you are here, or looking for the seer, or looking for the thing that is permanent, or looking for the certainty that you exist, if you will do this, or your own version of this, eventually you will get to the well. In the end, what you have to bring to bear here is your own natural intelligence and common sense. Once you get a sense of what it is you are looking for, that natural intelligence and common sense kicks in, and, although you may bang against a wall here, bang against a wall there, eventually you will get to the well.

Don't discard, disregard, or throw away any of the other things you are doing in your life (your education, your therapy, your physical therapy, your spiritual practices, your job), but just do this as often as it occurs to you to do so: just turn your attention backwards, determined to see yourself, for yourself, directly, without understanding or mediation, just for a second. If you will do this, over time, in ways that you won't even recognize, this false belief that you are your life alone will vanish. It will go away, and with it will go the internal warfare and this constant wellspring of fearfulness and anxiety that characterizes human life now. That is what I promise you. It won't be the way you have been conditioned to believe it will be, like "enlightenment", or "rapture", or anything like that, because, you see, it's really true what they have told us: just as you are, you are what you have always wanted. And, in the absence of this false belief that you are at stake in this life, the whole rationale for the internal warfare collapses, and your life reveals itself to be everything you ever wanted.

But first you've got to rid yourself of this lie, because this lie poisons the well, it poisons the life. It puts upon the life a burden that it can't carry. So, that's what I am here for. I am here to introduce this self-inquiry to you, if you have not heard of it; I am here to argue with you, if you have heard of it; I am here to encourage you, to trick you, to speak with you, to urge you, and listen to you, and fight with you about self-inquiry, which is an investigation of some duration. It is an adventure into what it takes for you to be satisfied, and for the whole issue to be gone for you.

I'm aware that what I really want is the fight, the war inside to be over, and I've experienced times when it was just gone.

Yes, we all have. That's the reason why we are so willing to believe that it is possible to do it, because we all have these experiences.

I see now that I can't have ideas about how it's going to unfold or look. But I still have a fight with that...

But you see, you can have ideas about how it should look and how it should go, because, well, can you stop having ideas?

No.

Of course, you can't. And the idea that you can't have these ideas is just more fuel for this internal warfare, right?

That's right.

Kill those ideas!

That's right, and it's exhausting...

All I am asking is that in the intermissions when you don't know what you are going to do next, do this: look at yourself. Look directly at yourself, look at what it feels like to be you, to be here, to be present, just that. And it isn't like a magic wand. That's what we want, but it isn't like that. You will get a glimpse, and it will feel really good. And then you'll go off talking about it to yourself, and this and that and the other thing... And that's okay, you don't have anything to say about that. None of that matters. None of the time that you spend talking about self-inquiry to yourself, or wondering how it should go, or certain that it should go this way, none of that makes a bit of difference. The only thing that counts are the moments, the seconds that you spend in direct, face-to-face contact with reality, that's all that counts.

The times when it feels like that's the case, I don't feel like I did anything for it to be apparent, for me to be aware of it. There were times when the time/space/mind...

Yes, but those times can't be instances of reality, because they came, and they were here, and then they left, right? They are instances of the spontaneously arising phenomena, all of these different flavors of spontaneously arising phenomena that we love, and hate, and are indifferent to, and so forth. That's just one of those. It's not bad...

I am still looking out there...

Yes, of course you are...

I am looking for something...

Yes, of course. But see, you can look out there, and still look at yourself. It's so common for us to say, "I'm still looking out there," or "I don't quite have it yet," which means that I'm not quite ready yet. But that's just a lie, that's all predicated on the belief that you are this life, and that just has nothing to do with you. Don't worry about it when you are looking out there. Just when it occurs to you, stop for a second and see if you cannot just look at yourself. Not in order to end the war here, but just to see the truth. Not in order to gain clarity, peacefulness and openheartedness, but just to see the truth. And then again, and again, and see what happens. I can't take from you all those other practices.

If there is a practice, it seems to bounce back from being hyper-vigilant, which feels like a lot of work, to noticing whether there is a willingness to see the truth...

That's assuming, of course, that you would recognize willingness when you saw it, and not take it for unwillingness, or wanting an ice cream cone... This is a mistake that we make: we think that the things that are going on in our heads have some validity to them, but they really don't. They are not hurtful, but they are not going to be helpful to you in the investigation. What is helpful to you in the investigation is this innate intelligence and common sense that doesn't talk about itself, but just naturally pushes you, points you in the right direction. You know it, you feel something is off when you want to be doing this but you are really doing that. You feel that something is off. That's that natural intelligence that doesn't talk about itself. And once you have made this turn, that same natural intelligence will guide you. You will resist it. If we could follow this natural intelligence, if we could only just relax and let it have its way with us, everything would be okay, but we fight and resist... But that's okay, too.

I feel that what you are talking about is just sort of a flow, and yet, there is still a fight. I feel like I am more and more in touch with that flow, and yet there is still such a strong fight. It's experienced as just extreme adrenaline inside, even though my mind may be quiet, there is a physical energy...

And that is directly resulting from this idea that you are this life alone. And there is no way you can be talked out of that idea. The only thing that will rid you of that idea is the truth, taken generously, and as often as you can. Well, of course, you know what it feels like, because you *are* the flow. I mean, it is not like the flow suddenly starts when you become enlightened, or whatever it is that you imagine is going to happen. The flow is flowing all the time, all the time. And you know, it doesn't matter whether we fight it or don't fight it, it's still flowing all the time.

So there is still a strong idea about how it's supposed to look...

That's right, but that idea isn't the problem, and it is so hard to see that. That idea is not the problem, that idea is a *symptom*. That idea arises from the conviction that I am this life and nothing else, and therefore, I'd better get things right in this life.

It's not working, but it seems to be a real strong conditioning.

Yes, and it's okay. It's not the problem. We are always trying to solve the wrong problems; we are actually trying to solve the symptoms instead of the problem. The problem is the lie. The solution is the truth. And the wondrous thing about this teaching that really differentiates it from about anything else is the fact that it is *verifiable*. If what I am saying is not true, all you have to do to find out that it is not true is to see if you can't see yourself.

So you are saying that being willing doesn't matter?

Being willing doesn't matter.

It doesn't matter what thoughts are arising?

What I am saying is that we don't even know what *willingness* is.

That's just a thought.

It's a thought, it is some energetic sensation that we think about and then we call it "willingness", even though we are thinking about an energetic sensation that isn't even here, it's something that we wish were here, you see? All of that can go on just as it does; I mean, it does go on just as it does. There is nothing in the world you can do to stop it. It will stop sometimes; it will come back some other times. Maybe it will go away forever someday, who knows? So that's not the problem. The lack of willingness is not the problem. The internal warfare against just relaxing and going with the flow, that's not the problem. None of that is the problem. That's part of the drama of your life, that's part of the fun of it. If it is anything at all, it is part of the fun of it. It is not the problem. The problem is the belief that you are this life and nothing else. And the solution is the truth, taken frequently. Okay?

Okay.

I'm glad you came up. One of the hardest things to do is to rid ourselves of the crusade that we are on to find the problem and fix it. "The problem is my lack of willingness," "The problem is that I am depressed," "The problem is that I am resisting the flow." We are always ready to ride out on a crusade to fix the problem. "The problem is that my mind is too noisy, I am thinking all the time," "I think too much, that's the problem," "I have gone to sleep, that's the problem," "I am in a trance, that's the problem." None of that is the problem. The problem is the belief that you are subject to all of that. That's the problem. But we are going to fix that. We are here to fix that problem, and you'll be so happy when it's gone! (*laughter*).

∞

When you invited us to argue with you, I immediately felt drawn to do so. It's a lovely invitation, and I find myself arguing with you about how hard it is. You said, "How hard can it be?" a few times. But it seems it is hard.

It seems that way. It does, it seems that way.

It is so easy to get tripped up, day in, day out. It is such a subtle practice, the things you are talking about, and it seems so rare that people practice it to fruition. So, it does seem hard...

I am not so sure that's true. I get a lot of reports from people who have been with me for a long time, and they report just exactly what I would expect them to report, if the practice had borne fruit. One of the things that have brought about such a shift for me in the last two years is the upsurge of these reports that I receive from people all over the world, who have tried this practice. And the reports are not like, "Oh, I get it, I'm enlightened, I am awake." The reports are exactly what I would expect from those who have lost the belief that they are nothing but their lives.

So, I don't think it is true. I think it has been true in the past, but I think that is because in the past we have always been stuck on these kind of half-stepping methods and practices — practices that quiet the mind, or bring intimations of reality by the triggering of samadhi states, practices of devotion, and other kinds of intellectual practices — none of which have done us the slightest bit of good. That's why our perception is that it is very rare, because it *has* been very rare. You know, we hear things such as, "Oh, that guy, who was it, Padmasambhava? He got it, right?" So we hear these stories, but they are few and far between. But I tell you that reality is so intimate, so inescapable, that once you start, you are pretty much doomed to go to the end.

And it seems hard, but really, for whom? What is hard about it? You are here, right? How could that be hard? It seems hard, but it's not; it only seems hard — until it doesn't. Because the truth of the matter is, what you are trying to see, you are always already seeing. That's the truth of the matter. Now, I know that trying to see it can *seem* hard, but I tell you it is not.

I want to know that and feel that, and I still don't agree with you. I want to agree with you...

Find the one who is reporting on this difficulty. That's the thing, always. This is another one of these circumstances where there seems to be *you* and *me*. But you don't know that, all you know is that there is you, and this conversation happening in consciousness. There is you and me, and this conversation, and you just don't see that it is easy, but you would be happy to find out that it is easy. All that is going on, the thoughts about it, the speech, the exchange with me, all that is going on, but who sees all that? From whence comes the report of all that? It's not from the thing itself, it's from something else. Rather than trying to resolve these conflicts, look instead for the *source* of this opinion that they are a problem. Look for who sees it all. If you look for the seer, I swear, you will find the truth. You won't find the seer, but you will find the truth. It is exactly the direction that the truth is to be found, that you are to be found.

It strikes me, as you speak, that the sense that it is hard is part of the internal warfare.

Yes, that's right. It is, and it's not a problem, even the sense that it is hard is not a problem, if you just do it. And this is a wonderful opportunity we have here. This is the whole point of a retreat like this. Well, it has a number of points to it, and it has some things that I particularly like about it, but the main point of the gathering together like this in retreat is to set aside this time to try to investigate what is true, what is real, what doesn't change. This is your chance. And come back later, and argue with me, after there is something really to argue about.

Am I allowed to ask you anything I want?

You are allowed to ask me anything you want.

How wonderful! So, it doesn't have to be like when I'm confused, when I have questions?

It doesn't have to be that, because I know you are not confused.

This is my first time being here with you in physical form. I saw your picture and I didn't want to come, and here I am... We are both wearing red, and that's pretty much the only reason I wanted to ask you a question. Why did you wear red tonight?

Why did I wear red? Because I was looking for a shirt to wear, and it was the only one that wasn't dirty, and might, you know, be kind of attractive...*(laughter)*

Because I imagined you wearing blue tonight.

I almost wore blue, but then I didn't.

Yes, well, I was just actually trying to be proper, and cover myself up, being a young female, so, I'm under cover...

Me, too.

Yeah, I can see that, and I love the fact that you have Ramana's picture here. Why do you have Ramana's picture here?

That's a good question, actually. You know, not long ago we were in Santa Monica and we forgot the table. We have another table; this isn't the one we usually use. We forgot to pack the table in the van. So, we didn't have a table to put Ramana's picture on, and I said, "Well, that's okay, let's just do away with that, we don't need a picture of Ramana. Ramana is dead, he can't do us any good now." So, I didn't have a picture of Ramana, and I told the people what I just told you: before you jump to any conclusions, we forgot the table in the van. But we don't really need Ramana, we are not here to talk about Ramana.

Then why is the picture here?

Because I like Ramana.

I do, too. That's a good reason.

I think people commonly don't get Ramana. Here's what you have to see about Ramana: he has a really great sense of humor. He thinks we are really funny. And if you see that, then a lot of stuff about Ramana falls into place. He's just kind of pulling our chain. In the end, Ramana always comes back to the same thing: Who are you?

Nithyananda is very similar to him, and he always comes back to the breath. I've never understood why masters would always go back to the breath. I thought, What's this about breath? This is so boring!

Breath ain't going to be here forever, you know? There is usefulness to the practice of watching the breath, but the usefulness has been lost with generation after generation after generation of trying to gain enlightenment by watching the breath. There is usefulness to it, but it is not that. It is more like training the mind, that's what it is. It is to make your mind clearer, and more agile, more supple, and that's useful.

Thank you so much. I guess that was my question: Why do we have to watch our breath?

You don't have to watch your breath. Look at yourself.

Absolutely wonderful. Thank you so much for being here.

You are very welcome. Thank you for being here. Okay, that's it, no more. We've got to call an end to this meeting. People are tired, I know that. We will meet together, you and I, eight more times before we go. One of those times will be in a small group meeting. We have lots of time. The most critical time is the time that you spend away from here, when it is possible for you to try this by yourself, because you are in this on your own. Later, I will tell you that is not true, but you are in this on your own. Here you have the time to try this, because you know, there are no experts in this field. There is nobody who can give you a seven-point, step-by-step procedure that will lead you to the truth of what you are and solve all your life's problems, and make everything right for you. But start tonight. When you go to bed, when you go to sleep, just take a second, as you are falling asleep, to see if you can find this presence that is never absent; just see if you can see what it feels like, this presence that you know is you, just as you are falling asleep. And then, in the morning, as you wake up, if you are fortunate enough to have a second or two when you are not quite sure what you are doing here, what you are about, just rest in that for a second. See what you are, before you gather together the thoughts about how the day is going to go, and what you are going to do. Just see what you are. Look at yourself. All the work is in the looking.

Enjoy yourself. Enjoy Ojai. Life is sweet. I am, again, grateful for you being here. I am grateful for your attention and time, and we are going to do good work here. Thank you.

Look At Yourself

Meeting 2

November 3, 2007 - Morning

Okay, good morning. Welcome back, I'm glad to see you. I want to review a little bit of what I was trying to get across last night. There are a couple of things I was saying last night that I really think are important to see. I don't think these things are necessary in the sense that if you don't see them or understand them, you're doomed to a life of misery and suffering, but I do think that there are a couple of things which, if you at least are willing to entertain the possibility that they are true, can make it easier for you.

First and foremost is the fact that self-inquiry, the direct investigation into the nature of what we are, is not a spiritual practice. I mean that very seriously; it is not a spiritual practice. There is nothing wrong with spiritual practices; some of them are quite useful and quite beautiful and quite effective at what they can be effective at. I am not saying that spiritual practices are bad and they should be banished and you should never sit and meditate or do pranayama, or any other kind of meditation again. I am just saying that self-inquiry is not a spiritual practice, and it is very difficult to see that, since it arises in such a spiritual context. But it is not spiritual. It is a practice that seeks to determine, first of all, whether it is possible to actually have the full knowing of the reality of our nature, and, secondly, to attain that knowing of the reality of our nature. It is a practice that leads to the destruction of all false beliefs about our actual nature, whether the false belief is that we are these lives, these minds, these thoughts, and nothing else, or that we are infinite, eternal consciousness.

The truth of what we are is not the actuality of what we are. Truth is a little bit loaded word, too. The actuality of what we are is not accessible to spiritual understanding, and it is not accessible to normal understanding, either. It is not something that can be discovered, packaged, described, and understood in the way that we are accustomed to understanding things. It's not like that. It's not a spiritual state, and it's not a non-spiritual state. It is not a state. You are not a state, never have been.

It seems difficult to divest spiritual viewpoints, understandings and practices from this inquiry, and one of the reasons for that is that the whole insight of self-inquiry, or *atma vichara,* is very ancient, and it has its roots in spiritual practice, in spiritual aspiration, and in spiritual attainment.

The atma vichara of the past was different from Ramana Maharshi's self-inquiry. In fact, Ramana's self-inquiry represents a really profound and fundamental departure from the atma vichara of Sankara, and all the other spiritual practices, whether they come from India, or Greece, or China, or the Holy Land. I may be wrong about this, but I can't find anybody prior to Ramana Maharshi who, in a spiritual context, suggested to us directly, face-to-face, that what we should be doing is making the effort to see directly the actual nature of what we are.

Most of the practices that appeared prior to Ramana and have gained ascendancy in the world of spiritual life have to do with what we have been doing all along, which is trying to make our lives satisfactory, even if "satisfactory" means making our lives enlightened, realized, and awake, which is, of course, the most radical kind of satisfactory life that we can seek after.

But even with that as the pinnacle, all of these practices are devoted to doing something to our lives — transcending them, transforming them, saving them, redeeming them — that will make them satisfactory to us, something that will resolve in us the causes of the fearfulness and anxiety that underlie most of our waking moments and reconcile us to the certain death of the body that is ever-present with us — whether we are denying it, trying to get away from it, trying to understand it, trying to get it, trying to get rid of it. The certainty of the death of the body, the death of the person, is ever-present with us, and most of these practices have to do with either reconciling ourselves to that, or persuading ourselves that it is beside the point. The same happens with all the rest of the issues that plague us as human beings in these lives, and these bodies, and these minds. Most of them, so far as I know, focus their efforts on the salvation of the life, the salvation of the person, the redemption of the person, the redemption of the life.

Ramana Maharshi comes to us with the simple suggestion that the problem is this false belief, and the thing to do about it is to look and see what you are, to resolve it once and for all, directly, for yourself, without any regard to what anybody else has to say about it. And this is the radical nature of the gift of Ramana having appeared in this world.

Now, it is certainly true that Ramana was a human being, that he wasn't right about everything, and that he wasn't perfectly adept at transmitting, offering, or teaching the power of what he had to offer us. He was a human being like me, like you, like all of us. But to actually try to receive and try to see what it was that Ramana presented to us is quite an adventure; and it is a surprise, because he is not what he seems to be.

So, it is important for me to, at least, communicate to you that, from my point of view, Ramana is not spiritual, and the self-inquiry or atma vichara of Ramana, is something new in the universe, because we have lost our way over these thousands of years. We have sentenced ourselves to lives of endless seeking, endlessly trying to get better, endlessly trying to get free, endlessly trying to get this, to get rid of that, to be this, to not be that. All of this with perfectly understandable and admirable intent behind it, but really, we have lost our way.

The truth is that we are not what we believe ourselves to be. We are not what we think we are, and if that problem is resolved, all the other problems fall.

So this is different. And it is not a teaching, or a practice, or a belief system that holds that everything else is wrong. It is not that the spiritual practices are wrong; it's not that they are bad, or evil, or sinful, or cause us pain and suffering, it's none of that. It's not that this is the practice that you must choose, and discard all your other practices, whether they are spiritual, therapeutic, religious, or anything like that. This has nothing whatsoever to say about those things. It has no position regarding those things. The inquiry is simplicity itself, and it is not so much that in the inquiry we discover what we are, because we always know what we are. There is never a moment when the seeing, the knowing of the reality of what we are is missing. So, it is not so much like that. We can get confused when we think the inquiry is about finding out what we are, because then we think it is about finding what we are in the same way we find out what butterflies are, or beef stew is, or energy is.

It is about exposing the false belief about what we are to the light of the reality of what we are. It is not about finding out anything. It is merely about exposing the lie to the light of the truth. And, in the light of the truth, the lie has no chance. And the result of this is — well, you'll see. We will talk about that as time goes on.

So, that part is easy enough to get across, I hope. The part that is almost impossible to get across is, how do you do it? I mean, somehow, it seems really, really hard to do it. Somebody I was talking to last night said it seemed really hard — and it really does. But the reason it seems hard is because what we know and understand about things causes us to look at what the mind has to say about things in order to figure out whether we are doing this right or not, so that the thought "This is very hard" is what we attend to, rather than the one from which this thought emerged, and about which this thought is thunk.

There is nothing wrong with thoughts such as "This is really difficult, you can't see yourself," "If you're seeing yourself, you're seeing an object," and "How do I go about doing this?" There is nothing wrong with those thoughts. But you do have a choice: you can put your attention on those thoughts, and try to understand them, and try to use them as a means whereby you can become effective in the inquiry, or you can just decline to do so, and, instead, with all your heart, with all your intelligence, and with all your common sense, for yourself, look to see if you cannot see yourself, with your attention, with your consciousness, with your mind's eye.

There are clues: you are permanent, you have never been absent. So, if you are looking for yourself, and you see something that wasn't here yesterday, it is not you. You are the same all the time. You don't change. You are unhurt and unaffected by any of the drama and the wonder of human life. You don't change. You are always the same. You are untouched. You are the same now as when you were three years old.

That's another clue: if you look for something that is in a state of flux, that sometimes is big, and sometimes is small, that sometimes is scared and sometimes is brave, that's not you. You don't change. You are permanent.

The underlying sensation, the underlying sense, the underlying feeling of presence never changes, it is always here, and it is as good a place to look for you as any. There is this feeling of presence, of just being present. And here is where we get into these kind of weird areas. It gets difficult to speak about, but you must see what I am speaking about. There is a presence here that seems almost to be apart from you, because you are so accustomed to seeing yourself as being apart from it.

But it is here; it is always here. It never changes. It is permanent, and it is you. This is what you are looking for. If you are absolutely certain you are here, look for that, look for the ordinary, what doesn't change, what is the same, always. And here is the deal: that looking is occurring from within the lie that you are this life. That is the reason why what you are seems to be apart from you. There seems to be some separation from you, because what is looking is a phenomenon that occurs within the lie that you are this life, this mind. Where else could it occur? You have no concerns whatsoever with becoming free, or liberated, or awake, or enlightened or any of that.

It comes from within the lie itself, and this produces the illusion of apartness between you and this always-here presence, this shining, silent, subtle, unchanging presence. So, the inquiry is to look at this presence, because this is the light, and looking at this presence brings the light into the lie. The point is not to gain some sudden, new and exciting understanding of what you are. The point is to expose this falseness, which is searching for a solution, to the actual truth of what it is, from whence it comes, to where it goes. And that is what does the work.

Now, the mind certainly will talk about it. It will talk about it, it will praise it, it will denounce it, it will say it can't do it, it will do all kinds of things. The temptation is to pay attention to the mind's talking about it. And the temptation is strong, because it is a lifelong habit of behavior. That's okay, it's not going to hurt you. But you have a choice: you can attend to all that talking about it, or you can look and see: is this presence, this reality, this underlying certainty of being here ever affected by the mind's chatter? Does it touch it at all?

So, always, in all cases, the opportunity is present to just look at this underlying reality. Just to look at it, not to get it, not to become it. That's absurd, since you *are* it. Not to get it, not to become it, not to understand it. Just to look at it, so the light is allowed into the darkness, which is the false belief that you are trapped in this body, trapped in this life, trapped in these thoughts, and desires, and stupidities, and brilliance, and wonders and horrors.

That's the inquiry. The inquiry is looking at reality as often as you can, looking at what you know to be unmoving, ever-present presence itself, as often as you can. And, as you do this, as it proceeds, you will see that it gets easier, and the whole idea of it being difficult begins to disintegrate. It gets easier and, in fact, it is so wondrous a thing to be doing, that you will find yourself wanting to do it all the time. This is what is meant when it is said that the inquiry takes over, or that the guru within is calling you. The guru within is you, and as you begin to look at yourself, it will become clear to you that this is really pretty much all you want to do. I mean, I want to do all of this other stuff, too, but not if I can't do *this*.

So, the purpose of this retreat (even if you have been doing this for years) is, in your spare time, in your off time, as we are sitting here, as you are listening to me, to begin to just take a second every once in a while, and see if you can't catch a glimpse of this underlying, unchanging, ever-present reality. It's ordinary; it's what you are seeing all the time. You are never not seeing it but, to begin, whenever it occurs to you during this time together, just look: I am here. I am.

And don't concern yourself with spiritual understandings. You don't need to get rid of them, you don't need to follow them, and you don't need to not follow them. Don't concern yourself with the nagging, niggling problems of your life, or your health, or your livelihood. I mean, don't concern yourself with the fact that they are present. Don't concern yourself with the fact that you have to think about them, or that you do think about them. Just don't concern yourself with any of that stuff. You don't have to stop thinking about that stuff. You don't have to stop trying to do right. Just when you can, in the midst of all that trying to do right, in the midst of all that trying to understand, just stop for a second and look at yourself, let the light in. Just open the door a little bit. Let the light in. The light cures it all. The light fixes it all.

See for yourself. One of the main features of self-inquiry is that you see for yourself. If there is any truth to it, you will see it. If it is just another trip, you will see that, too. Trust yourself.

Trust your own native intelligence, your own common sense. It doesn't take a philosopher, it doesn't take a Buddha. It doesn't take any of that. It just takes the natural intelligence that arrives as part of this life, and the common sense that also arrives as part of this life.

There has been a perception shift for me and I really have gotten that I am not my life. There's like a grokking. It is hard to even put it into words, but it is like the body and the stuff that I was concerned about, the patterns and neurotic stuff don't seem as important as they used to.

That's an authentic report. It's not that it is fixed necessarily; it's not even that it needs to be fixed necessarily. It is just not quite as important.

So, the kind of excessive concern about all of that stuff is dropping away a little bit in what seems to be a larger context of what I am. I have an awareness of what doesn't change, but it is also becoming kind of non-local. I am also becoming bigger.

It is always non-local. It's your vision that is becoming bigger. That's good news. You know, there is no way that I can talk you out of this stuff. That's the other thing about all the spiritual practice and therapy. It is true that it's not as important, and all that, but there is no way I can talk you out of that. This is a side effect of the inquiry. This is a consequence of the inquiry, the realization that the problems that plague the life are really not the problem. And the idea that causes us to want to fix the neurotic behavior, because if I fix the neurotic behavior, everything will be okay, that idea kind of vanishes. It is not that it can't be fixed, or shouldn't be fixed, but it is just that I am not at stake in its getting fixed.

The urgency and the idea that if I don't get it, that drive...

That's right. That fades…

What I am seeing is that stuff is still going on; they are just sort of patterns that are associated with all of this. And I see that they are still happening, but it is just not the problem that it was before…

That's right. And, surprisingly, you will discover that in the absence of your death-grip on these things, they resolve themselves. It takes some time, but they resolve themselves. They are, after all, only the consequences of past action. Not just your action, but your action certainly adds to them. And, in the absence of you acting on them, they kind of fade, they kind of fix themselves.

I think Papaji said something like not to engage, but it is like the wrestling with them keeps them going, and the identifying that as me and I have got to fix it…

That's right, it is a self-enhancing routine. It's interesting that you said that about Papaji. I don't know what to say about Papaji. Papaji was like an explosion, and I am very grateful for having known about Papaji, and being with people who were very intimate with Papaji. And the thing about Papaji, and also about Ramana, is that they are just like the rest of us. The light of reality may very well destroy and disintegrate the false belief that causes the misery and suffering in their life, but it doesn't mean that they suddenly know everything, or they do everything right, because they are just like us. Just like you. The same patterns are here, still playing as the life.

And all that to say that this encouragement, "Don't engage in these things" is fine, but it is pretty much useless. Like "Don't attach to this," "Don't get caught up in thought." It's all fine, it's like telling you to be what you may or may not come to see as your real nature, in time, but they are not much use, they are not much help. How do I go about not engaging in this horror that has been causing me such distress and such discomfort for so long? How do I do that? Well, you can't do that. The engaging is part of the process; it is part of the pattern itself. And the good news is, you don't have to disengage from anything. That happens on its own accord, once the light of truth is let into the whole murky darkness of this idea that I am trapped in this life.

What seems to be happening is that the concern about it is dropping away, so the disengaging is just organically happening, and it's not that big a deal...

Yes, that's right, that's what I am saying. It is just an organic part of the process of disintegrating the lie, the disease. It is a disease. It doesn't make you bad, it doesn't make you good, it doesn't make you stupid, and it doesn't make you smart. It is just a disease, it is just a virus we caught somewhere.

And so the 'I' arising out of that... I am also kind of seeing it wanting to come up and claim lots of stuff. But that is all part of what is happening, and sometimes it does, and sometimes it doesn't...

It doesn't matter, either way. Really, it doesn't.

I am seeing that. I don't wrestle with that, either...

It's very surprising. Once you have been doing this for a while, and especially if you have a deep spiritual background, you get really surprised at the things that just kind of happen on their own, and really don't matter. I really don't have to figure out how to not engage in this neurosis, or I really don't have to figure out how not to be so concerned about the outcome of things, I really don't have to do that. It's okay if the "I" is taking credit for reality, that's okay. It doesn't hurt you, it doesn't touch you, it doesn't change you, and it doesn't affect you. If you just continue the inquiry, all these things will take care of themselves. This is something Ramana said again, and again, and again, and it used to really bother me. It seems like every time he was speaking to somebody, he would finish up by saying, "For whom is this problem?" or "Who are you?" or "Who sees this?" Then he would say, "Just do it and everything will turn out all right."

But that's the truth, that's what you are reporting. If you just look at reality, everything takes care of itself, over time. These lives are time-bound. It's not like they can be corrected in one fell swoop. Over time, all these things take care of themselves, once you see that they are not doing anything anyway. This is really good news.

For a long time, when you said "You are not your life," it was like there was a "Yeah, but..." But that just kind of disappeared.

It's the inquiry.

There is a question, though. I already know what the answer is, but here is the question. There are some times when the stuff seems to take all the space, and I forget...

That doesn't matter.

Yeah, I'm starting to see that, too.

Yes, you see that, too. That just happens. It is part of the process. And, because you can say "sometimes this happens", you see that it happens. And then, it doesn't happen. You don't know it's going on when it's going on, because it takes up all the space. But then, when it's over with, you say, "Oh!" And maybe you could say, "Good riddance!" Or maybe you could say, "God be with you!" Whatever, right? But it doesn't hurt you. Okay?

Thank you.

How can it be that this that has occupied my heart and soul and every bit of intelligence that I can muster for all of these years can turn out to be best left untouched? How can that turn out to be? And, if I tell you that that's what it turns out to be, if I tell you you are not your life alone... Well, you already know you are not your life. That rings true somewhere deep down in the dungeons of wherever it rings true, but the response is, "Yes, but..." And what that points out is not that you are wrong because you say, "Yes, but..." That is not the point at all. The point is that the effort to persuade you that you are not your life is a waste of time, and the effort for you to try to take in the intellectual understanding that you are not your life, that is a waste of time.

That is a consequence. That doesn't give you anything, except more things to chew on and worry about. The only thing that does you any good is to look at yourself. That's the only thing that works in this realm. Other things work in other realms, and god bless them. But in the realm of finally being finished with the belief that there is something you have to do, something you have to get, that there is something wrong, something off, something that needs fixing, this is all that works. This is it, there is nothing else: look at yourself.

Let the light do the work. You know, light disinfects. Sunlight disinfects. The light of reality disinfects this kind of festering false idea that I am my life, and that I am trapped here, and that I am at stake here, and that I have got to do something or I am going to go to hell, I am going to die, I am going to go to eternal torment. I am in eternal torment. In this realm, this is all that works.

∽

Hi, how are you? I heard you got work.

Am I tired!

I'll bet. It's tough. But you look good.

It just seemed like the practical thing to do.

Of course, it is. How can you not get work?

I fought it, because all I wanted to do was this...

But work doesn't interfere with this.

No, and yes, because I forget.

If you forget, then you must remember, too.

Yeah!

There it is. It doesn't interfere with this.

Yeah, it's weird, you know?

This is excellent. This is a good thing to have come to you.

I am here. I mean, I am here!

I know you are.

I am staying at the monastery. I have a beautiful room there, and when I walked in and I sat down on the bed, it was like, 'Here I am! Here I am!' Different room...

But still... The room is in you, not the other way around.

Like this room. This is it!

That's right. It is in you. This body is in you.

There is nothing else.

That's all. Nothing but you.

That just blows me away!

But it is true. I say, 'There is nothing but you anywhere to be found', and it sounds like this is some big spiritual pronouncement. But just check it out. You can't find anything but yourself anywhere. You will find all these things that come and go in you. It is all you.

It's so simple. But I still try to make it complicated, with all the 'But what about this? But what about that?'

Yes, but you see, that is not you trying to make it complicated. You have never tried to make anything complicated. That is just this mechanical apparatus, this set of conditioned responses, conditioned arisings, and spontaneous phenomena appearing, and it has nothing to do with you. There is no need for you to stop trying to make it complicated. That can only cause you misery and suffering, because the fact is that you are not involved in making it complicated. You are the container of it, that's all. And it doesn't hurt you. The effort to make things complicated that are simple doesn't hurt you. When you remember, just check and see, 'Am I here?' That does all the work. And it doesn't matter whether the tendency to make things complicated stays or doesn't stay. It doesn't change you. It doesn't hurt you, and it doesn't help you. You are the same.

The point of that is not to get the fact that you are the same, and the fact that you don't do these things. The point of it is only to look there, so that this light can come into this life, into this mind, and finish the work of destroying this false idea that you are this life. And then, the effort to complicate the simple may continue, or it may not. What is that to you?

It seems like that false belief is disintegrating...

Yes, I think it is. I see that.

Not completely. Sometimes, it's complete, though. Sometimes it is complete, it's just gone...

Yes, right, right. Sometimes, there is no sign of it whatsoever, and then, it kind of reconstructs itself, and that's okay. The real truth of the matter is that even the false belief isn't a problem. It really isn't because, even for all of the time that you were caught and trapped in that false idea that you are this life alone, you remained the same. It really didn't hurt you. So that, although it sounds like we are trying to get rid of that false belief, that's really not it. The disintegration of the belief about what you are is a consequence of looking at what is real. It is not a checking and seeing if what is false still remains, but looking at what is real.

It almost seems like it just happens...

It does.

It's just like you are there...

That's right, that's what comes as a result of trying to do it over time, and that is what I was talking about earlier, when I said that it takes you. This is what you want to do. This is what you are here for, to look at yourself, for god's sake. Why else would you create all this drama out of you? And now you get the straight stuff, the pure water, and, of course, you are going to go back to it. You are not going to have to think about it. You will be caught up, you will forget all about it, and then you will come back, and you will say, "Ah! Here I am!"

And that's what does the work. That is what does the work, not anything else. It is just those moments of clear seeing that do the work. And those moments of clear seeing come as a result of the first beginning of the effort to find that clear seeing. And then, once you have seen it, it's easy. How could it not be easy? You are here. Always.

I was asking myself, 'What does it feel like to be here?' And it feels like this!

Yes. That's right.

This is what it feels like.

That's it. That's it.

This!

I am happy to see you.

I'm really happy!

I see that.

Today was about the best that I have heard you speak. It was really good! It was really good!

Well, actually, it ought to be, right? Really, it ought to be. We have this idea that spiritual teachers spring full-blown from the forehead of Zeus or something, with absolute, clear understanding of what they are talking about, but that is garbage. This is my life's work. This is Carla's and my life's work, and we are learning as we go along. Our life's work is to bring this amazing possibility to you, and we learn as we go. And, if the last time I said something isn't the very best, then I am not making any progress, right? *(laughter)*

When I first heard you, there was some little something that I knew what you said was true. Then I thought, I better not jump to conclusions… I better keep coming back. Thank you!

Oh, you are very welcome. It's useful to come back. It really is. It is useful to speak about these things together, to reflect on them together. When you are by yourself, especially in the beginning of the inquiry, especially in the first year or so of the inquiry, it is really easy to fall back into the habit of taking seriously all the thoughts, and all the ideas, and all the falseness, and to feel as if you are trapped, even though the truth is that if you continue the inquiry, all of that will go away.

But, if you have the chance, and we can get together again, come back, and let's look at it freshly. But if you think that you can just believe this and go on about your business, then I am not doing my job. There is nothing to believe in this. It is a great gift to me that people sometimes really hear that what I am saying is true, and then come back to wrestle with it, and figure it out, and so forth. But if you think that just believing this is true is going to rid you of this falseness that has prevailed for thousands of years, then you are probably on the wrong track. So, come back.

Keep up the inquiry. If you can't come back, keep up the inquiry. Even if you think you are doing it wrong, keep up the inquiry, because, in the end, you can't do it wrong. As long as what you are about is trying to see the truth of what you are, you can't do it wrong. There might be some more skillful ways to do it, and some less skillful ways to do it, but you can't do it wrong. So, if you can't come back, keep up the inquiry. And if you can come back, come back, and keep up the inquiry. I love you, I really do. You are quite a gift. Thank you.

Thank you.

∞

I just wanted to talk a little bit about doing the inquiry, and sticking with it. Thoughts have been out of control today, and I have seen that. Sometimes I feel like I am really resting and doing what I would want to be doing, and that feels right, and it feels permanent, it doesn't seem to change. I just wanted to check in with you today.

I know that sometimes we say things because we are trying to say something and we don't say it quite right, but most of the time what we say is a clue to something, right? So, I have to point out to you that the point of the inquiry is not to rest in it. I mean, it is natural to think that that would be the point, that there will come a time when I will just be resting in this kind of sweetness, and lack of concern, and permanence. But that is not the point, and that is an example of a mistake that we make a lot, which is thinking that we need to get something we don't already have, that things have to be different than they already are.

So, the point of the inquiry is not to come to the point where you are constantly resting in quietude and equanimity, and so forth. The point of the inquiry is only to look at you. That's all. You are never absent from this equanimity. There is never a moment when it is missing, even during the darkest times of your life, even during the times in your life when everything was hopeless, and you hated the world, and you hated yourself, and you hated your stupidity. Even then, you were resting in this reality. You never leave it.

So, what happens in this inquiry is that we do find these states. They are states because what you have found may be permanent, but your relationship to it is new. And it is the relationship to it that is impermanent, this state of resting in it. So, we get these states where we are resting in a kind of dispassion, equanimity, and sweetness, and all of that, and we think that is what we are after; we think that what we are going to get in the end is to make that kind of state permanent. But that is not the case; it is just not the case. That is what we are, already. We are already resting in that state, always; we are resting in reality, always. The activities of the mind are beside the point.

The activities of the mind may prevent you from doing the inquiry for some finite period of time, but, like everything else, that comes and goes. That comes, and then it goes, and you can return to the inquiry. But the inquiry is not in order to bring you to some new state of being that is a permanent state of peace and equanimity, because that is already the case. No matter the appearance, that is already the case. The point of the inquiry is to destroy the false belief that you are subject to the state of resting in being or the state of being captured by thoughts and their ugliness. Do you follow that?

I do.

That's good, that's really good. That is a really excellent question to bring forward.

I really want to find myself. Checking in and doing the inquiry, sometimes I will have the thought, 'I'm here,' and I will end it with just that thought that I am here, instead of actually doing it. It's kind of taking the placebo instead of the medicine.

Yes, right, and that's okay. The problem is not that. The predispositions of every individual are completely different, so that the difficulties that arise during the course of the inquiry are unpredictable. In some cases, the underlying characteristics of the difficulties are predictable, but the way they manifest is unpredictable. So, that's not a problem; the fact that you take the placebo is not a problem. Just, whenever you can, take the medicine. And you don't do that by concerning yourself with ridding yourself of the inclination to take the placebo; you do that simply by taking the medicine, every time the opportunity presents itself and you really can see that there is this chance for you to just get a glimpse of yourself. Just do it, because that does the work. Not the doing away with wanting to take the placebo, not doing away with any of that stuff, not doing away with resting in being. It is the looking that does the work, over time. Okay?

Thank you.

Is that helpful?

Big time!

Okay. That is what I like to hear. And this is the kind of usefulness that can be had from us getting together and talking about these things, because what he perceives to be his problems is what everybody perceives to be their problems. "My problem is that I don't do it right," or "My problem is that I am not resting in being long enough," or "My problem is that I take the placebo." That is not the problem, none of that. All of that is beside the point. The problem is the belief that you are this life, the belief that you are subject to, and affected by, any of that; that you are helped by resting in being, and hurt by taking the placebo; that you are helped by resting in this sweetness and love, and you are hurt by not being able to control the mind's endless aggression. It is just not true. And the point of the inquiry is to determine whether or not what I say is true. You do the work, and then tell me if I am lying. I can't persuade you of it. And if I could persuade you of it, I wouldn't. You have got to see it for yourself. Anything else?

Okay, then. Enjoy yourself. Do the inquiry. There is no "right time" or "wrong time" to do the inquiry. Standing in line waiting for food is as good a time as any because it is the looking that does the work, not the looking in a certain setting. It is the looking that does the work. Not prolonged gazing, but just a glimpse out of the corner of your eye subtracts from the load of false belief.

I am really happy to be here, I am really happy to be with you in this adventure. Thank you for this meeting.

Look At Yourself

Meeting 3

November 3, 2007 - Afternoon

The first thing that has to happen in order for us to effectively embark upon the investigation into our nature is that we have to see what is called for. This is more important than it might seem. I don't know if this is true of everybody. But I know that, in my own experience, in my own life, when I happened upon the idea of the spiritual solution, I immediately concluded that there were no experts and that I could figure this out for myself. And what I mean by that is that since what we are talking about is the reality of things, and they all say that we are that, the only one who could possibly concoct a method whereby I could weave myself through the traps, and the thoughts, and the stupidity, and the conflicting desires, and so forth, was me. And furthermore, this would be really easy. How hard could it be? This would be really easy. I would just dive right in and there I am.

It turns out that it is not as easy as it sounds at first. There are definite steps. In order to be effective in the inquiry, you must see that you are the one that has to do it. You have to see that. I mean, maybe you don't, maybe you can flail about for two years like I did, but you will be a lot better off if you begin by seeing that you are the one that has to do this. That is why I bring this suggestion to you. You will be a lot better off by seeing that the goal of the inquiry is not the transformation of your life. It is not the ability to be able to finally rest in the sweetness of being. That is not the goal of the inquiry. So, to start out with, you would be well advised to see that you have got to do this for yourself. There is no real book of directions that comes with it. And the goal is not what you think it is, because we think we know what we are talking about. Especially when we get into this spiritual business, we know what the goal is. The goal would be, if I am to say it, the transformation of this life, the redemption, the salvation, the fulfillment of this life, the clearing up of the wrongheadedness that is my nature, the gaining of clarity and clear seeing and understanding of reality. Any of us, when we get involved in the spiritual world, it must be for the same reason we get involved in all of the other realms: to fix our lives, to make them better. It is the same with the spiritual realm. We get in the spiritual realm to fix our lives finally, to make them better, the best they can be, to clear up all the garbage. So, when we happen upon this that really is kind of the last resort, the final possibility, we naturally think that the purpose of this too is to transform my life, to make me happy and peaceful, to perhaps rest in the bliss of being, to rest in peace. Now that doesn't sound so good, does it? *(laughter)*

But that is what we want. That is what we think we want, to rest in peace. So, along with the recognition that I have got to do this for myself, it is extremely helpful for you to see that the purpose, the goal, the reason for the inquiry is not any of that. It is not to transform your life. It is not to make you peaceful and blissful, and ever sweet, and gorgeous, and beautiful, and so forth. It is okay if that happens, but that is not the goal.

The goal of the inquiry is to look at yourself. I can't tell you how hard it is to get this across. The goal of the inquiry is to *look at yourself.* Period. The outcome of that is beyond your control, beyond your ability to foresee, beyond any usefulness for you to try to foresee. The goal is to look at yourself, as often as you can. That's it. There is no other immediate goal to the inquiry. And it is quite useful if you try to take that seriously when I say it, because I promise, you will save yourself a lot of heartache and a lot of headache. You can go ahead and rest in peace, and be blissful with all those other practices. That's fine, no problem with that. But you are going to have a much easier time of it in the inquiry if you at least consider the possibility that that is not what the inquiry is for. The goal of the inquiry is to look at yourself, that's all.

Now, the reason we undertake the inquiry is to rid ourselves of this lie that we are something — life, mind, consciousness, god, love, hatred, anything. It is to rid ourselves of all beliefs about what we are, so that we don't rely on belief anymore, and we know firsthand, without mediation, without the need to understand or explain, the reality of what I am. That is the reason we undertake it.

But the goal of the actual work is just to look at yourself. That's all, just to look at yourself. The eradication of the lie has its own consequences in your life, which no one can predict. With the people that I have been with all these years, and in my own experience, and Carla's experience, although it is impossible to predict what the outcome of losing these beliefs will be in detail, the outcome seems always to be better than it was before: an improvement in the life, which is actually quite strange, and there really is no reason why that should be so. But it does seem to be so. I am going to talk about that some more, a little bit later in the retreat.

The goal of the inquiry is to look at yourself. Now, there is no way to tell you how to look at yourself. I mean, as I have said already several times during this retreat, I can try to trick you into seeing yourself, and I can try to talk you into looking at yourself, and I can share with you my own experiences in this regard, but there is no road map, there is no way anybody can tell you how to look at yourself. Even to say it, reveals the absurdity of the proposition that I can tell you how to look for you. Because here you are, there is nothing anywhere to be found but you.

What I can tell you is that once the investigation, the inquiry, the seeking is undertaken, once it is taken in by you as something you want to do, it teaches itself. Once you start trying, *it teaches itself.*

So, what I want to do is get you doing the inquiry, and that's all. That is all I want. All I want to come out of this entire retreat is that everybody in this room leaves this retreat doing the inquiry, according to their own predispositions, just according to what they are, and how their particular personality plays out. I don't want you to be enlightened, you can't get enlightened. Enlightenment is not on the table here. Realization is not on the table, awakening is not on the table. That is inaccessible to you. That is not possible for you. That is a fool's game. It is what gets us hooked up. And it takes us nowhere except here, to the question, *Who?* or *What?*

So, I am done — by which I mean, do you have anything you want to say to me?

Yes? It seems like it has been a long time since I have seen you.

It has been a long time.

It's good to see you now.

It's really good to be here. I never know what gets me here.

I never know what gets me here, either.

But I needed to be here. I have missed you, even though you are always with me. Since I did those two series of five-week meetings with you, something has really changed. My life is exactly the same life, but the eyes I am looking through are not the same eyes. And it was really funny, because all you ever said during those small group meetings was, "Every time you think of it, just turn your attention inward to look at you." And what I am seeing now is that it is not about finding. It is a simple living with that, frequently turning attention inward. That is so hard to put into words. There is something that loves being looked at, something that really responds to being looked at, and is so happy that it is being looked at, that it just feels like it bestows something so generous. And I may sound vague, but I don't know how to put words to it.

One of the problems that come when we are trying to put words to it is that we try to project upon reality a personality, a personal identification. And of course, that is what we do all of the time, anyway. But that is one of the problems that come when we try to describe what reality is like, because we anthropomorphize it, like we do to everything. But we don't know any better. What do we know? But the truth is that reality doesn't bestow anything on anybody. That's the truth.

That's the experience...

That is a story about reality, but reality doesn't bestow anything other than everything. But that is true anyway, even if you are caught in the trap of the belief that you are this life, and suffering every minute of every breath you take.

I just saw something as you were talking.

The life itself is not alive. You are alive.

The life itself, without the self-inquiry, felt so dead to me, really dead.

Yes, that's right.

I don't feel dead anymore. I don't feel scared anymore, either. And since I am not so invested in the life, and I am not taking it personally, I am enjoying the hell out of it.

·

Isn't that a surprise? You would never expect that from the spiritual teachings, would you?

No.

Really, you never would expect that from the spiritual teachings. The spiritual teachings have life held at arm's length, like "It's a dream." "It's a Leela." "It's something out there." "I am beyond the need to care one way or another."

It's amazing when that self-consciousness falls away. My life is not what I am. There is nothing to do but enjoy it. There is nothing to worry about. The other thing that I wanted to say, before you started talking about it, is that what has been so much in my awareness is that it all exists in me.

That's right.

And, it's so humbling.

Yes, it is.

It should be the opposite of humbling, but it is so very humbling.

Yes, of course it is. The only entity which can express humility or pride is this inert life itself, this thought 'I'. And certainly it is humbling to the sense of me as 'I' that it all exists in me, including 'I'. It all is you.

It is critical to see directly for yourself that you are not your life — you are not the mind, the thoughts, the desires, the consciousness, the hopes and aspirations,. You are not your history; you are not your future. It is critical to see that. And this is the sword that self-inquiry is, the sword that you wield by looking at yourself, because the truth is that it is all you. There is nothing but you, nothing but you anywhere to be found. So, it is actually all you: the stupidity, the ugliness, the aggression, the hatred, the lust, the compassion, the love, all of you.

And what is so interesting is that it's not a problem.

And it is not a problem, that's it.

I spent so much of this life so disassociated, and it was like a really fine distinction beginning to experience the difference between being disassociated and not attached. And it's not a subtle distinction, but I had to experience it to know it is not a subtle distinction, because one is dead and the other is alive.

Yes, that's right.

And I am so happy to be here with you and talking to you. It feels like being here also is getting a tune-up.

Tune-ups are good.

Tune-ups are really good. And you know when you came in last night, and you just glanced in my direction briefly, and I looked back, it was like, "Where is John?" What I was looking at was so vast. I don't even know why, but I couldn't stop the tears from streaming down my face.

All you are ever seeing is you.

And I know that because you are in my life. Honestly.

Well, I am very happy to be in your life. I am very happy to have this effect on you.

Thank you.

⌒

So, doesn't anyone have any problems?

Why not tell us some of your experiences?

Oh, I don't know. Many people have heard many of my experiences, because I am not shy about talking about myself. And then, there are all these podcasts, and videos, and stuff out there, so a lot of people have heard pretty much everything I have to say about my experiences. The one way I can characterize my experiences as a spiritual seeker — and I think this is universally true — is that everything that I could possibly do wrong, I did wrong. Every way I could possibly be stupid, I was stupid. Every possible way that I could avoid, postpone, put off, delay and sabotage anything happening in this life, I did.

And it is this that gives me the energy to want to be helpful to you and to get you to inquire, above all other things. It took me a long time before I would even consider such a thing as the self-inquiry in the manner of Ramana Maharshi, because it was beyond me. It was too simple for me, too elementary. It was for people who didn't know what *I* knew.

First, above all else, I want to get you to do the inquiry. And next, in any way that I possibly can, I want to be of service to you in helping you be more intelligent about it than I was, use less of a brute force method, and have a little more subtlety and intelligence about it. But above all else, I want you to try the inquiry. I want you to look at yourself.

I want you to take encouragement and enthusiasm from the recognition that the possibility of seeing yourself and ridding yourself of the false belief about what you are is real, and it is not some airy-fairy spiritual thing. It is very real. It is very practical, extremely practical. The goal of all the spiritual aspiring in our entire history is in your hand. All of the wonder of the Buddha, the realized ones, the enlightened ones, and the sutras and the shastras, and everything that has been written about reality, is written about you; and you can see for yourself where all that came from. It is in your hands. You don't have to do anything to get qualified for this. You don't have to be initiated. You don't have to be given any special teaching, any special transmission. It is you. It is all about you. The whole history of spiritual aspiration is about you. I want you to see that. I want you to see that it is not for the Buddha, or for Sankara, or for Ramana Maharshi. It is you. It is about you. And I want you to see that the only thing that makes it seem that life is so miserable and so horrifying is the belief that the life is you, that all there is to you is this life. That belief can be wiped out by you. Not by me, by you.

So, my experiences aren't really all that useful. If I tell you my experience, sitting, trying to kill off ego, trying to do this, trying to do the other thing, I fear that you may try these things on your own, and they are really not suited. Don't try this at home. *(laughter)*

And if I tell you some of the magnificent, blissful, paradisiacal experiences that were inflicted upon me prior to being tossed into hell, where I actually *needed* to find the truth, that isn't going to do you any good anyway, because if you haven't had those experiences, sure to god you will want them. And if you have had them, sure to god you will want them back.

꩜

I am happy to see you.

I am happy to be here. It has been a while. You asked if any of us had any problems… Well, I guess I do.

There we go. That's good.

When I do self-inquiry, when I look at myself, more and more, not only is it revealed who I am, but it also reveals some of the thoughts that I guess you might call them "defects", the things that have run my life, that have created the misery, created the suffering. There is a part of me that tells me to disregard them, that they are not important, and to just focus on who I am. But there is another part of me that tells me I must change them, because they are what I have heard since day one, from everybody around me, and then myself…

Right… Be a better person.

Yes, and they create suffering.

Well, they don't, really. That is not true; they don't create anything, really. They are themselves the outcome of suffering, and past action, and all of the circumstances in which they appear. They are reactions and responses, they are not creators. They are in fact inert, and can't do anything. Let me start with the beginning of what you said.

The goal is *not* to reveal who you are. You said in the beginning of this, "more and more who I am is revealed." The goal is not to reveal who you are. This is really hard to hear. The truth is that there has never been a moment in this entire life when you have not been seeing the reality of your nature. That is not really new. So, the report that "more is revealed of the truth of what I am" comes from just a story. That is not the goal. The goal is just to look at yourself, that's all.

The idea that these negative thoughts, and negative intentions, and negative actions are the cause of suffering is also not true. They are the suffering itself, in the form in which you are seeing them. The cause of suffering is the idea that you are at stake in what happens with these thoughts, and that these thoughts are you. That is the cause of suffering. The root cause of suffering is that false belief. So, given our life history and our life experience, and because it is the common view that these negative intentions, thoughts and projections are the cause of suffering, it is quite natural to conclude that what I need to do is do away with these thoughts. But that never works. That is just one more movement of hostility and aggression, trying to kill off these thoughts.

It really is natural to assume that, to think that. It just doesn't happen to be true. The thing that eliminates suffering is eliminating the belief that you are this life. And the belief that you are this life is unseen, unconscious, and, in fact, it is the lens that you look through. You can't see it; you can't see the cornea of your eye. That belief gives rise to a deep, equally unseen conviction that *I am at stake here,* that it is really important that I get this right, and that if I have bad thoughts that seem to be causing suffering, before everything else, I have to do something about them, because I am at stake here. This is *me,* you see? And it's that at-stakeness that gives rise to this undercurrent of anxiety and fearfulness, out of which comes all suffering.

So, I tell you that is the case. I tell you that is the case in order to persuade you that it is okay if you keep trying to get rid of these thoughts, it doesn't matter. That is not going to hurt you; it is not going to help you, either. It is okay if you think that the thoughts are causing suffering, that too is beside the point. What I want to persuade you to do is not to rid yourself of the idea that those thoughts are bad, or to rid yourself of the thought that they are the cause of your suffering, but merely to look at yourself so as to bring the light of truth onto that lie that you are your life. The outcome of this action will be the disintegration of that lie, over time, and the end of all misery and suffering in this life, the snuffing out of the anxiety and fearfulness. They come from this unseen conviction that I am at stake here. Then you will see that those thoughts aren't what you think they are. And your badness is not what you think it is. And in the absence of this hostility, aggression, and internal warfare, even the thoughts get sweeter.

If you are not vigilant doing this inquiry, it is easy to fall back in the void.

Yes, that's right. You have to keep it up. In my experience, the thing that differentiates between those who persist in the inquiry and those who drift off is that those who persist in the inquiry have had the actual, conscious experience of seeing what it is that I am trying to point you to. And it seems to me that once that conscious experience is had, it is actually impossible for you not to look at yourself. You can go for a long period of time forgetting it, but eventually you are going to come back to that well.

So, the important thing in the inception of the inquiry is to really satisfy yourself that by means of this internal investigation you actually have had a glimpse of what it is that I am talking about, of this presence, this silent, unchanging, never absent presence. This can seem separate from you, just because of the deep seated belief that you are separate from it, that you are something other than it. But that seeming separation from you vanishes very quickly. You are looking for what is permanent. You are looking for what doesn't ever change. You are looking for what you are always seeing. I mean these to be kind of clues, so that if you see it, you say, "Ah, I see what he is talking about." Are you following me?

I think so. It is glimpses, and I have had those glimpses.

Right.

But then I fall back into the everyday stuff again.

Well, maybe you have to be more disciplined.

Probably.

I had it lucky, I had it really lucky. I came upon the urgency of resolving this in prison, where I didn't have anything else to do. That was great good luck. So I did this, because I was desperate, and didn't have anything to distract myself with. Well, it is a little bit more difficult for you because you have a full life, you have a rich life, and it is easy to be distracted, since it has been distracting you for so long.

So maybe what you need to do is set aside some time, and sit down, and just relax. If you know some simple watching-the-breath meditation, do that, just to settle your mind. And do this religiously. Do this every day. Find the time, sit down, relax yourself, calm yourself. Because you know what you are looking for, because you have had these glimpses, right? And look for it. Look for it.

I think you are absolutely right.

You need to do that, I think. You need to apply some discipline to this. Take a time every day. It doesn't have to be a long time, just long enough to see it. It could be five minutes, just long enough to actually get that glimpse again. Take a little bit of time, sit down, watch your breath, settle down, and resolve that you will look at yourself. Move your attention inward and backward, looking for that which is always here. And when it comes, go on about your business.

Thank you. I needed to hear that.

I think that it is useful, I really do. I don't often think about discipline. I probably will think about it more in the future because, as I said, I didn't have the need for that, because there wasn't anything else to do.

Yes.

Let me suggest this to everybody. Take time every day. Sit down. It doesn't have to be a long time. Sit down. Relax. Close your eyes. Settle your mind through whatever means that you know to do so, and then look at yourself. Do this every day, as a practice, if you will. As a practice, every day, sit down and look at yourself. It can't hurt you.

That is all I really want, it is for you to do that. I am getting more willing to speak about these matters in down-to-earth practical terms, and to provide some practical advice for how to do it. This is what I did. I sat down as often as I could and I did a watching-the-breath meditation. And then I would see if I could not see the one who was seeing all of this, the subject of all of this. I would turn my attention backward, like looking through the back of my eyes. And I did a lot of things in these sessions of practice that were pretty ridiculous. But I didn't care, because I was desperate to be rid of the ugliness of this life.

∞

Thank you for sharing just now some of the practical aspects. I just really had a great desire to look into your eyes. That is why I wanted to come and sit here next to you.

Well, there is nothing special there. It is just you.

So I will look into my eyes. Thank you.

You are very welcome. I tend to be not much on this looking-into-the-eyes business, though I like looking in your eyes. I don't know what the reason is, but I tell myself the reason for that is because there is such craziness around in spiritual circles. There is such craziness around, where there is this convention that something is transmitted, especially from the guy who is sitting up here to those who are sitting down there; that there is something to be transmitted through the eyes. I really can't transmit anything. Cross my heart.

It seems like you have become such a clear mirror, more so every time I see you. So that it is not like staring into somebody's eyes, but it's like a mirror. You are so clear, we can see ourselves. It could feel like a transmission, but that is what it seems like to me.

In any event, to me, that is all kind of mumbo-jumbo. I can't help it, it is the kind of guy I am. *(laughter)* I don't have anything against it, but this is so contrary to what it is that I am offering. What I am offering is the suggestion that *we all are adult and intelligent enough to find the truth for ourselves.* Maybe we need some help, maybe we need somebody to point us in the right direction, and to give us the benefit of experience, but really, we are in this on our own, and there is nothing I can do for you. All that I can do for you I do when I say to you, Look at yourself. Or, maybe I do some more by talking to you, but very little. It is up to you. You really have got to do it for yourself. I can't zap you. I can't take away the false belief about what you are. And I am not suggesting that any of this was happening between you and me, but I just love the opportunity to talk about this stuff.

What about when Gangaji looked at you, and you had the experience? I've had a lot of spiritual experiences in the past, one of which is what you are talking about. I've had many other types of experiences along the way, but I have never lost that identification with my "I" thoroughly. I had a spiritual teacher who gave me many spiritual experiences like Gangaji gave you, where they look at you, and you are just there. For ten years after that I could feel this vibration, there was a detachment, there was bliss, but there still was identification with myself. How did the experiences you had with Gangaji fit into all this? I would love to hear more exactly what you did, because all I know about you is up until you met Gangaji, and that she looked at you, and you fell in love with her, and who she was...

Oh, I fell in love with her. Let's not pretty it up. Don't spiritualize it. I mean, I did enough spiritualizing of it myself during that period, all right? *(laughter)*

I don't know what happened after that, and I would love to know. And I would love to hear about those experiences, because that is the kind of experience I had with my teacher, and I have been with him for thirty years, but I feel like I am going nowhere at this point.

It is a curse.

Well, it is nice being in love.

It is a curse. And it may be a necessary curse, but if it is a necessary curse, it is also necessary to abandon it.

I have prayed to never leave, because when you see those things, you never want to leave. Do you know what I mean?

Yes, but those things leave. There is an endless up and down to that. It is like an adolescent love affair, the spiritual explosions, and bliss and all that.

I hope that my experience is what you are talking about, because my experiences were of incredible bliss, but there was also detachment and wisdom...

Yes, and they come and go. That is what I mean by that. The wisdom, and detachment, and dispassion, and the clear seeing, along with the excitement and the ecstatic out of body experiences, they all come and go, and leave us bereft in their absence. And it is that aspect of it that I speak of as being like an adolescent love affair. It is so exciting. It is so wondrous. It is such a kiss from the universe. But it doesn't stay.

It stayed for a long time, but I haven't gotten to see my teacher for about twenty years.

"Long time" means that it doesn't stay. Short time, long time, they both mean the same thing: it doesn't stay. And it is a commonplace spiritual insight, at least among the Buddhists, that one of the most exquisite forms of suffering is the suffering that comes to the one who has everything they want, because of the underlying certainty that this has appeared, and therefore will disappear. So, these spiritual experiences, these wonders, these insights, these clear seeings are a curse, because they are so seductive.

And you feel like you should be in that all the time.

Because it is so obviously what you have been looking for all your life. But it turns out it is not. And this is, again, a way in which it is appropriate to speak of it as an adolescent love affair.

When you are an adolescent, and you fall in love for the first time, there is nothing but that. There is no possibility of being talked to about it; there is no possibility of any kind of rational consideration or reflection. It is the whole universe, and it has taken you totally, without your will. And it is the same with these wondrous breakings open of consciousness that produce the enlightenment experience, the realization experience, the awakening experience, whatever name you want to put to it. But, like the first love, it is doomed to leave, no matter how long it takes, no matter what circumstances have to be present, it will go. It is not what you are looking for. It is not. Now, with me and Gangaji, I am sure that my experiences were the same as yours.

It sounds like it.

I wrote to her every day, and twice a day sometimes. And she wrote back to me pretty much every day. And I spoke to her of my experiences, like my experiences of the stones singing silent arias of being… Really, that was my experience. It was as if those cold stones were singing to me silent songs, arias of being. And I knew, throughout all of that time, that I had gotten it, that Gangaji had given it to me, that she had bestowed upon me the goal of the ages. She had bestowed upon me enlightenment, realization. I knew that. And men in the prison started coming to me for advice, and I guess, transmission, which I was happy to grant. *(laughter)* But, throughout it all, if I had reflected upon it, I would have seen that something stank, which was easily seen by how important it was to me, how energetically I would get together a letter to write to Gangaji, how breathlessly I waited for her response. How proud I was of the way in which she had fallen in love with me. I was her pet. I was the proof of her realization.

Of course, when caught up in an adolescent love affair, reflection is not on the table, but if I had reflected upon it, I would have seen that there was something not right there, that it was too important to me; that it did not conform to what I had learned in my careful reading of the literature about what it was to be finished with the search; that it was far too full of me; and that there were these other things going on, like I really wanted to have a relationship with a woman. I mean, Gangaji was Gangaji, right? And actually I would have been happy to have a relationship of that kind with her, but that was out of the question. I really wanted to have a relationship with a woman. I wanted to be in love. I wanted that, and I denied it because that is as unspiritual as you can get, right? At that point, I had been in prison for about fifteen years, you know? I mean, really! *(laughter)*

And finally, the opportunity came for me to be in a kind of a romantic, unconsummated, sexual relationship with a woman; and I jumped on it. I said yes, this is what I want, this is it. And I can be enlightened, and all of this, but I want this woman. And I knew that this was fraught with some kind of wrongness, that there was something wrong about the whole set of circumstances. It didn't sit quite right. I mean, for one thing, the woman was married, and, for another thing, I only could see her in the visiting room of the prison. And for another thing, she was very close to Gangaji, and we were keeping it a secret from her. So, all of that added to the sense that it wasn't quite the cleanest thing going on there.

And then Gangaji found out about it, and cast me into the outer darkness. She turned her back on me. She would not have anything to do with me anymore. She wrote me once, and she started by saying, "Whatever it is you think you are doing, no matter how pleasurable, no matter how justifiable, stop." And I wrote back to her, and I said, "Well, why didn't you tell me that before?" She told me she knew all this was happening. Why didn't she tell me to stop before, if she wanted me to stop?

Things just degenerated from there, they went downhill. And this is the point of it. This isn't true romance confessions that I am trying to give you here. What happened then was that I found myself in hell. I mean the most horrendous, tormented, self-inflicted, childish, infantile pit of self-pity, suffering, and misery that I had ever known in my life. I hated the day that I had met Gangaji. If I had it in my power to do something about it, I would go back and never have that happen. I would go back to the time prior to her appearance in my life, when I was kind of a tough convict toward the end of his term, playing tennis, smoking dope and kicking it with the fellas. I would have done anything to undo my meeting with Gangaji. I would have done anything to forget about it, and go back to the way it was before. But I couldn't. There was nothing I could do that would break me out of this pit of suffering and misery. I couldn't find anything to do.

I had, of course, heard of Ramana Maharshi. I knew that he was kind of the root of this whole non-linear lineage of Papaji and Gangaji. I knew roughly his story as a sixteen-year-old boy, getting overwhelmed by the fear of death, and lying down and pretending to be dead, and being finished in the end of that. I knew something about that, and I knew that self-inquiry was what he taught. And I thought I knew what self-inquiry was. I knew that it was contained in the question "Who am I?" which is the title of the first thing that was ever written that is purported to have been dictated by Ramana. And I knew that this was not for me; this was for beginners... But I wasn't a beginner. I knew. I had a clear understanding of what I was. I had a clear understanding of the nature of non-dual reality, as clear an understanding as you can get. You know you can't really understand it, but I knew what it was about. I knew what was what. I knew that I was awareness, I knew that. I knew all of that. So, of what use to me could simple Ramana's simple question, "Who am I?" be?

But finally, things got so bad, my internal hell was so intense, and so unremitting, and so hopeless that lacking anything else to do, I turned to Ramana. I had already been involved in all kinds of spiritual stuff and that hadn't done me any good, and here is Ramana constantly coming back to my consciousness, so I turned to him. I got a copy of the book *Talks with Sri Ramana*

Maharshi, and I carried it around with me wherever I went. I read it again, and again, and again, and again. I tried with all my heart to get what it was he was trying to say. I just couldn't seem to make much sense of him, but I tried. And some of the things he said were very spiritually counterintuitive. One thing that always caught me was that he would advise people to hold ego by the throat, and not let go. This is supposed to be the shining light of our time, as far as advaita and non-dual realization are concerned, and he is saying something stupid like "get ego by the throat". We all know that ego doesn't exist! But it caught my attention, and I finally decided that I would try that.

I would sit on my bunk, and I would close my eyes, and I would get one-pointed with my attention, and I would move my attention looking for any object within the scope of my consciousness that felt like me, by which I mean small, contracted, mean-spirited, selfish, greedy, and stupid. And I would settle on something that felt like that, and I would tightly hold it with my attention.

I knew, of course, that that was all nonsense, but I was so desperate that I didn't care. I would hold this experience, this feeling, tightly with my attention. And, since I was there already, and since what I really wanted was to rid myself of this thing, I would take the opportunity to try to project upon it a death wish. Die, I would say. Die. Die. For a long time, again and again, I would assume this relationship with some innocent body sensation, and command it to die. Because of my advanced spiritual understanding, of course, I thought that the key to happiness was the death of ego. So, as long as Ramana had me holding onto something that looked like ego, I was going to kill it off. Die. Die. Filled with energy, murderous energy. And I did this for weeks, months.

One day I was doing it, and, in the midst of it, between one "Die" and the next "Die", it just hit me: "This thing ain't never gonna die!" *(laughter)* And I laughed and laughed...

See? This is what I mean when I say that telling you these experiences doesn't really give you much help, because I was really dumb. But the fever broke, the whole feverish insanity broke in that moment. And the possibility arose, finally, of actually performing the inquiry, of actually beginning to look for the reality of what I am, of actually beginning to hear from Ramana a different instruction.

Ramana, toward the end of his life, had cancer on his elbow, and that is what killed him. And I guess he was going to the doctors during the last days of his life. He was very sick and very near the end. He came from a visit to the doctors, and he spoke to the people who I guess were in the hall where he met with them, and they asked him, "What did the doctor say? Are you going to be okay? What is happening?" And Ramana said, "Well, they tell me I am going, but where would I go? I am here."

That got me, because it felt like what he was saying was that this person, this personality would survive physical death, which is so unspiritual, so not in keeping with the advanced non-dual understanding that we all have and are so proud of. It stopped me, and I reflected on that, and, finally, it occurred to me that he wasn't saying that at all. He was merely saying the literal truth, that *here* is another name for me, that *here* is what I am. It is not that "I", a being, am here, at some location, but I AM HERE. And then I saw that *I am here*. Yes, that's right. Here I am. If I want to find myself, I can just as easily look for here, look for what *here* is.

What is it to be here? What does that feel like? How do I know I am here? How can I be so certain? But I am here, I am here. Not here in this room, but here. And the rest, as they say, brings me to you. Which is why most commonly I ask people, Is it not true that you are here? Just look and see if that is not true. Now look at that again. And keep looking at that as often as you can. Because I can tell you, from my own experience, whatever brings you to see the reality of what you are, this seeing of the reality of what you are will destroy all the false beliefs about what you are, because truth is the only thing that can destroy the lie. And it is the seeing of this that does it, it truly is. It is the opening of the window for the light to come in, because it is the light that fixes it. And it is the looking that brings the light.

It took me untold time and agony to get there. I really advise you not to go through the same. It is really not necessary. It is not necessary to have spiritual experiences, it really isn't. It is not necessary to get rid of spiritual experiences. It is not necessary to go to hell. It is not necessary to not go to hell. No matter what seems to be occurring, no matter what is taking your attention within your consciousness, you are the same. You are this silent, shining, unchanging, eternal presence that is the source, the ground, and the container of it all, the space in which all of it comes and goes. And you already know that. The trouble with instructing in the practice of looking at yourself is that what I am trying to get you to do is try to see what you are always already seeing.

Was that helpful?

Yes, thank you.

☯

I feel like I am going back in time now. When you talk about inquiry being the goal, and the only goal...

The looking is the goal. The goal of the practice is the looking. Because if you assign some other goal to it, like getting to be peaceful, or filled with equanimity, or happy, the only way you can tell whether that goal is being reached is by looking in this life, by looking at the state of your thoughts, whether you are having wicked thoughts, or good thoughts, or sweet thoughts, whether you are being selfish or selfless. That is the only place you can look to see whether that goal is being fulfilled, which is a clue that that is not the goal. The goal is just to look at yourself. And everything else is taken care of, because the looking is the opening up of something that allows the light in. Now, there is no instantaneous transformation as a result of this, but the lie cannot persist in the light of reality.

Even if you are doing it wrong?

Even if you are doing it wrong. Because you will find out how to do it right. I promise. You already are fine, I know you.

I like the way you don't use the word "spiritual", because it is something that has always kind of bothered me. I cringe when I say it, and sometimes I want to describe these meetings to my friends, because everyone should come, at least once to see, and I don't even know how to talk about it. I just have no idea. And they don't like the word "spiritual" either.

I know, and I have the same problem. We used to call these meetings *satsang*, although we are losing that word as we go along, because I really don't want to bring people in on false pretenses, on the idea that we are going to do something spiritual here. But the Sanskrit word *satsang* means, approximately, association with truth. And because of that meaning, it has come to mean all the devotees getting together at the feet of truth, in the form of the guru, which is not what this is. Now, how you talk about that to your friends is a mystery to me, except for this: everybody wants something they don't have. Everybody wants something they don't have, and imagines they are deprived as a result of not having it. Everybody is unhappy. The purpose of these meetings is to get rid of unhappiness. It is a very practical thing. The purpose of these meetings is to see what is real. How about that? It is to see what is real, to find out what is real, and what is not. I would like everybody to come, too.

I don't know a lot about your background, and I didn't know why you had gone to prison. I know you were an activist of some kind. And when I am talking to my activist friends, to even try to talk about these things with them, even though I feel like it is at the heart of what they are doing, I could see them being really skeptical.

Well, I was a convinced Communist revolutionary who robbed banks and destroyed property in order to empower and encourage the working class to take control over their own lives. In the course of that, I did a number of bank robberies, a number of sabotage operations, and I spent two years on the FBI's Ten Most Wanted list. I escaped twice. I spent eighteen and a half years in prison. And there is some value to that, in reaching out to people. There is some value to that history, because that history is not what you would expect to find going to a meeting like this. *(laughter)*

You are special, John.

So, you can tell them that.

This might convince them. (laughter)

Tell them the guy is a gunfighter.

Thank you for the story, it was great.

Do the work. You've got to do the work. There is no savior that is going to come down from on high and rescue you from ignorance and suffering. You've got to do the work. The cause of ignorance and suffering is a false idea about what you are. It is really that simple. It is all about identity, all of it. And the solution is not to find some new identity to assume, but to find the truth of what you are. And then you can play all these other identities all you want, bank robbers, gurus, saints, sinners...

But you have to do the work. You have to take the time to look at yourself, and it is as Ramana always said: the course of this is always according to the predispositions of the individual. For some, the problems that I had and that I communicated to you, and that I try to help you not have, they never even arise. They just go, "All right, I see, I get it. Wow, sure glad that's over." And for others it takes longer... I haven't met anybody yet who is quite as bad as me, but I am kind of the other end of the scale. And you probably fit somewhere in between that. But you have to do the work. You have to. You have to look at yourself. You have to. And it's not hard. It just *seems* hard.

You are here. You are always here. You are never absent. And if you look at that, whenever it occurs to you to do so, you will find out for yourself whether there is anything to all this. You will find out for yourself what is real and what is not, what is worthwhile and what is not. And you won't have to be told by anybody.

Okay, my friends, I will see some of you in a little while, and the rest of you in the morning. Thank you for these meetings. I am so grateful for you, really. You are wonderful. You are fantastic.

Meeting 4

November 4, 2007 - Morning

Good morning. Welcome. I am happy to be here with you. I hope everybody slept well, and if you didn't, I hope you took advantage of the opportunity to look at yourself.

Yesterday we talked about a lot of things. The main thrust of what I wanted to accomplish yesterday was to speak with you about my claim that if you want to be finished with misery and suffering in your life, if you want to be finished with fear and anxiety and internal antagonism and the whole internal warfare by which we seek to fix our lives and our minds, if you want to be finished with all of that, in the end, the only way to accomplish that is to come face-to-face, nakedly, with the reality of what you are; and that the reason that is so is because the cause of the misery and suffering is the false belief about what we are, and coming face-to-face with the reality of what we are destroys that lie, over time.

The way in which this inquiry (someday I will think of a better word than that) unfolds in your own consciousness, in your own life, in your own mind, is entirely unique; it is entirely according to the predispositions of these personalities, these individuals. Because of that, it is not possible to say, "Okay, assume this meditation posture, and chant this mantra, and contemplate this particular object of meditation." The actual inquiry itself relies upon your own natural intelligence and common sense, your ability to discern when you are caught in the wrong direction, and to see that you are on the right track when you are going in the right direction. And that is what the inquiry depends upon.

I have tried to make as compelling, convincing, and persuasive as possible my sense that any attempt to understand what you are, or to find the solution to the problem of what you are in spiritual utterance is foolishness, and it is doomed to fail. The spiritual teachings, the spiritual utterances, the poetry, the songs of yearning and confirmation have brought you to the inquiry, and now they are done. They can't help you beyond the point of bringing you to the inquiry.

In all cases, in all practices, in all traditions, the inquiry is the end of the road. It is always the case. Everything leads to this. Everything leads to this only question that really matters, which is "What am I, really?" It is the only thing that really matters. I have told you, and I will tell you again and again: in the end, face-to-face with the possibility of the direct perception of reality, you are absolutely on your own. Nobody can go there with you, nobody can take you there, and nobody can tell you what you will see.

I *will* tell you that the repeated, direct perception of reality, in your mind, in your consciousness, will infallibly lead to the destruction of all beliefs about what you are. And that will lead to the end of misery and suffering in your life. But you have to do it. Nobody is going to come down from heaven and give you this. People, beings, creatures, gods, goddesses may or may not come down from heaven and be able to bestow upon you boons of samadhi states, and paradisiacal experiences, but no one can come down from anywhere and give you this certainty of the reality of what your nature is. Nobody can do that. You are on your own. You can get help, but you are on your own.

It is amazing to me that this practice, this possibility, is so hidden away. It is amazing to me that the whole species doesn't see this, and be finished with all of the stupidity that our species is so famous for. It amazes me that there is a view abroad that the practice of self-inquiry is for the few, and that it takes a lot of preparation, and a lot of I don't know what to get to it. It is for all. It is especially for you, since here you are.

I am going to be talking about something else this morning, but before I get to it, does anybody have any burning issues, or questions, or disputes about what we have done so far?

Is there any proof that the root cause of misery and suffering is misidentification, other than your own experience?

You must find this out for yourself. The proof is the vanishing of misery and suffering, as a result of the inquiry. The proof is in the reports of those who have tried it and who report the same thing, again and again, about the surprising easing off of the whole dramatic entanglement with the events of the life. There are a lot of reports about that. But that is not proof, really. The fact that I say it, or that some of these people who have done it say it, is not proof. The only proof you can have is by doing it. Now, the good news about this is that this isn't something like taking the Kool-Aid, where you are making some terrible, dangerous step. This is asking you only to look to see what you are, so there is nothing lost if it turns out to be false, you see? But the only proof is in the pudding, it is in the doing, it is to see whether this works. And the only way you can know that is by doing it.

When you talk about the false belief... Are not all beliefs false?

Yes, they are. That is why I most often now say *all* beliefs about what you are. This destroys *all* beliefs about what you are.

So, in order to delouse the belief, you experience the truth...

That's right, that's exactly right. Truth does it. It is the only thing that does it. All the rest of it is preparation and postponement.

I think I had a concern with the use of the word "truth". If you eliminate the word "false", and you just have the belief that I am my life, then if you experience what it is that you are, even the word "truth" is superfluous.

71

Yes, that's true. It is not so superfluous when presenting it to people who are unfamiliar with the practice itself, and with the underlying reality of it. But yes, they are superfluous.

Good. Thank you.

Actually, all my words are superfluous. But it is true that when I say "truth", I sometimes kind of cringe... But "truth" has a nice ring to it. And what I want is for people to come and find out what this is about. If I trick you to come by saying "truth", then you can find out what the real deal is. And "truth" is a nice word, but it is just superfluous.

The only thing that is happening in the inquiry is that you are looking at yourself, you are looking at reality. That is all there is to it. And the outcome of it is for you to find out, really.

◌

I am happy to see you, I am happy you are here.

I am grateful to be here. You just said that if you have a burning desire to get rid of fear, and anxiety, etc., then the self-inquiry is the way to go. And yet, you are also saying that that is not the goal.

The goal is to see what is true, what is real, what is actual. Actually, the goal is just the looking. Again, words are really difficult in this venue, but they are all we have. What I mean by that is this: at the point where you are actually engaging in the inquiry, in the moment when you are actually turning your attention, trying to see the actual reality of what you are, *the only goal is the looking.* The goal in this looking is not confirmation of what you believe yourself to be, or the attainment of peace and tranquility, or the destruction of misery and suffering, or any of that. It is those things, those larger goals that bring you to the inquiry in the first place, but when you are actually seated, or standing, or doing whatever you are doing and turning your attention toward yourself, at that moment, the only thing that you are trying to do is look. Do you follow me?

Yes, I do, and I am listening, too. And because I am in a little struggle, currently, in the back of my mind, I am looking with a goal. I want to get rid of this shit, already.

That's okay, too. But just at the moment of doing the actual act, in order to get rid of all that stuff, what you have to do is just be trying to look, trying to see that which is real. If you pull into the inquiry all of the misery and suffering in your life that has brought you to the inquiry in the first place, it diffuses the strength of your concentration and your attention. You are just trying to look, in that moment.

Okay, so my next question is, I have actually experienced who I truly am, and in many different ways over time.

You are never not experiencing what you are, but yes…

That's true. But there is a great difference when you really fully experience that everything is the same, that there is no difference, there is just one energy thing and you say, "Wow! All right!" And then it fades, and then you are back… And I am in a place currently where I am reeling, and judging, Wow! How do I snap out of this? I am really off! So I am grasping, I am trying to figure out what happened. Oh, yeah, I didn't keep up my practices, and so I have got to go back to that… And it just so happens that even when I am looking now at "What am I?" that stuff is still behind, so I am not quieting down yet. So what I am hearing you say is, "Well, this is the way, if you do this…"

That is not what I am saying. I am saying there is nothing whatsoever that is wrong or needs to be abandoned about any of the practices you are doing.

Then let me change my question, because I know that. What I am hearing is, "If you do the inquiry and you experience what you are, then it is over." But I have been there, and it is not over!

That is not what I am saying, either. I am glad, this is good. The inquiry is like medicine. The experiencing of the reality of what you are, well, you are always experiencing that. There is never a time when you are absent from that. The experiencing of it in the context of spiritual aspiration or attainment or in the context of just getting a hit of this wonder of the reality of what you are is fine. It takes repeated instances of the deliberate perception of reality. I know that this is contrary to the expectations that we get from most spiritual teachings. But it is not something that strikes you like a lightning bolt and finishes it off. It is something that incrementally, over time, disintegrates all beliefs about what you are. It is like light disinfecting a room, or like medicine healing a disease. It is not that you see it and that is the end of it.

I realize that I had that concept, and that every time I am off, I feel like, What happened?

Yeah, that's right, "I lost it…"

I like the idea of the clouds being thoughts, and then either you look and you identify with them, and then you are lost, so that you always have to be fully present. And the practices, like meditation, the things that I do, help me stay focused…

Meditation practices and things like that can be very helpful.

So, are you saying those practices are great, don't let them go, and keep up the self-inquiry? Is this a lifelong thing?

The inquiry? It already has been for you, you just don't know it.

So, is witness consciousness the same thing? Just witnessing?

No, it is not. Meditation practices can be useful, especially in calming the mind and giving some strength to your concentration, and some suppleness to your ability to focus your attention, so that some of the craziness is kind of quelled and doesn't attract your attention. But they are not inquiry. The inquiry is only a momentary seeing, without understanding or naming, the reality of what it is to be you — this background presence that never moves, that is never absent, that never changes and is unaffected by any of it, and may *seem* to be separate from you. This is the reality of what you are, and it is the determined, conscious intent to look at that, just momentarily, repeatedly, that is the inquiry. It is the repeated part of it that does the work. It is cumulative, it is not like we have been led to expect, somebody coming out of the clouds, or some internal thunderbolt striking and clearing everything up, and making everything right. It is not like that. It is destroying all beliefs about what you are, and it takes time. And there is nothing whatsoever in any practice that you are doing that interferes with this.

So, when you say "It takes time", what are you really saying?

I am saying that the disintegration of the lie takes time.

And then it's disintegrated, one day...

Yes. Actually it is gone, generally speaking, before you know it is gone.

Then you can consciously keep up the intention to do inquiry.

Yes, of course, yes.

So, it's a part of conscious living.

That's right, that is all part of conscious living. When the inquiry does its work, what is missing is this underlying sense of anxiety and fearfulness, of being at stake in what is happening here. That is what is missing. You live your life the best you can. You be as conscious as you possibly can. You pay your bills, you take care of things, you do all of that, but without the sense of the possibility of some imminent disaster if you don't get it right, if you don't have the right thoughts, if you don't have the right intentions, and so forth. And the whole world breathes a sigh of relief when that happens.

I'm seeing that all it is about is keeping that practice consciously in the moment. I am seeing, and experiencing, in looking back as you were speaking, that it is just consciously doing that inquiry.

That's right, that is all it is. And what makes something that is so easy seem so hard is that what you are trying to do is trying to see what you have always already been seeing.

Well, that's what I have been doing the last 24 hours, because I really haven't done that before. And I am just saying, "Okay, I know that." And then what comes to me is that it is just so subtle, it is like noticing that now I am consciously looking... That's right. And then I say, "Oh, all right, so you are just addicted to drama and fear, and they are just little addictions," and then I get caught.

Those are insights, and insights will come. But those insights don't fix the problem.

No. They never do. And then I have to go back.

That's right. The problem is the false belief, and the only thing that does away with that is looking at reality, repeatedly, over time. Your insight and your diagnosis of what is going on in your mind are probably accurate, but nothing we have ever tried to do to make the mind sweet and clear of neurotic impulses has ever worked. So, what this does is just remove the suffering from it. It doesn't mean that the neurotic impulses are going to go away. These things are conditioned behaviors that have appeared over a long period of time in response to many circumstances. And once this engine of warfare, which is the belief that I am my life and I am at stake here, once that engine is gone, these negative, neurotic impulses will, over time, relax.

I have been there a long time. And now I am back, and what I want to say is that there is a part of me that is tired of this. It is just this loop, you know? And then the only response I have to myself is, "Well, you never kept it up consistently, there were breaks, and you fell through the cracks." But now I am back. I am going to keep it up consistently. I am kind of tired, you know?

And this is where you come when you are tired. You come to the end of the road. I promise you, if you undertake this inquiry seriously, with commitment to it, everything will be taken care of, everything will work out. And if you do it, you can find out for yourself whether I am lying or not.

Well, I know what you are saying is true, because I have been there. And so the only reason I am talking like this is because I am in that state...

That's okay. I am very happy to have you here.

Thank you, I am grateful, thank you.

ᄋ

This is a question from somebody here who doesn't want to speak. Is that right? You want to continue being silent? So, let me read this letter first.

> You tell us we are not our lives. You tell us when the lie is destroyed, life is sweet. My question is hypothetical: Carla leaves you without much explanation as to why. Within a few months, she is happy with another man. Where is John, then? How much of this are you not? Is life still sweet now? Is nothing at stake then?

Oh, I don't know, I might go murder the guy! *(laughter)* And if I did murder the guy, life would still be sweet, then. You see, when I say that life is sweet, I don't mean it is easy. When I say that inquiry brings an end to misery and suffering in your life, I don't mean that it brings an end to pain and discomfort, and distress, and hard times. What it brings an end to, totally, irrevocably, is the belief that you are your life. If your life is difficult, the absence of the belief that you are your life means an absence of the misery and suffering that usually attends difficulty — being jilted, being cast aside, or being stolen from, being assaulted, being raped, being whatever. It doesn't change the nature of the play, the nature of the drama within the context of the life. I can't possibly tell you what I would be like in a circumstance like that. If I were to make such a claim, you should throw me out of this room. No one can tell you what such and such a set of circumstances would produce, and what kind of a response it would produce.

Actually, this is a good time to move into the rest of what I want to talk about today. Let me tell you for a minute just how I see things, what John Sherman looks like to me, what this life looks like to me.

Everything I see, everything without exception, every experience — every tactile experience, every olfactory experience, every visual and auditory experience, every thought, every emotional arising, every body sensation — that is all John, all of it. You, here in my consciousness right now, that is John. This is all me, which is, of course, exactly the way you see it from your point of view, although it may not be apparent to you that you see it that way. Every circumstance that comes to me is John. Every bill that cries out to be paid is John, everything I see is John, so that the nature of John is constantly in flux, it is shrinking, expanding, shifting, changing. It won't hold still, actually. There is neither rhyme nor reason to it.

As we sit here in this room together, it is as stable as ever. It is never any more stable than it is during the time that we are spending in this room together. We are all in the same place, things are not moving around too much, the context that we are appearing in is kind of set and stable, and John is kind of stable.

But when I leave this room, John becomes something wholly different, he becomes the totality of the perceptions, and the relationships, and the interactions that will affect me then, as I walk out the door: the sunlight, the heat, the traffic, the car, the sound of the engine, and so forth. This is all John. This miraculous marriage, that is John.

But John is always changing, always shifting. And sometimes, there are times when problems and hardships become part of John. Payroll taxes that I don't have the money to pay, past due personal taxes that I don't have the money to pay. The rent is due tomorrow, and fortunately I do have the money to pay the rent on time this month, but sometimes I don't. My cat has, on several occasions, had serious, terrible injuries that had to be attended to. This is all part of John. The memory of this is part of John, always shifting, always changing. I have problematic relationships with some important people in my life. That's all part of John, all part of this life, all part of the ebb and flow, and shifting, changing nature of this life. Always changing, always different, always something new comes, always something old comes back.

The thoughts that come to me, old, conditioned responses in reaction to circumstance. When I watch television and I hear about what this country is doing in the world, and about the plight of humanity in the world, old, conditioned responses to that reappear: the desire to do something about it, to punish the evildoers, to stop them from doing what they are doing. They freely come, and go. All of this is John: anger, fear, hatred, all of this. Old conditioned patterns of reaction, old neurotic responses to circumstances, all coming and going.

Much of the apparatus of protection and aggression has, over time, lost its strength; it's a will-o'-the-wisp now. But it is still here, still playing, still part of the apparatus that is John. Speaking to people, doing the inquiry, listening to people, hearing their reports, being filled with the delight and the gratitude for the things that I hear from people about what the inquiry has done for them in their lives, this is part of John, also. The certainty that I am not doing this right... I could go on and on...

Everything that happens, everything, just like you might imagine yourself to be, just like you — except for one thing. All of that, in all of its coloration, all of its distinct characteristics, all of its ugliness, all of its beauty, every bit of it, without any exception whatsoever, *there is no resistance to it here.* That is gone. Resistance is gone. I have no idea what would happen in such a fraught circumstance as Carla leaving me for another man, but I do know from my experience that there would be no resistance to whatever came, even if I did murder the guy. All of it, every bit of it, every second of it, every nanosecond of it, every breath, every heart beat of it is absolutely delightful.

We are so unbelievably lucky to be born human. We can't conceive or comprehend the great good luck of being born human, until we rid ourselves of the *idea* that we are human. I don't know, no one can know. But, maybe uniquely, we are conscious of ourselves as conscious entities. It is a miracle. We have the capacity to engage in this drama of life, this magnificent play of life, fully, without holding back, without resistance. We see things, we hear things, we smell things, we touch things, and we *know* we do. We have the constant movement and sensation in the body as it does what it does, as it functions, as it breathes, as it pumps blood, as it digests food, as it has pain, as it has relief from pain, as it has pleasure. We are endlessly conscious of the body, and it is like a magic shop of experience and wonder. And it is all John, every bit of it.

Now, I have looked, and you can look for yourself; see whether there is any possibility of finding a boundary, a place where your mind is not. See if there is any possibility whatsoever of finding a boundary that shapes your mind: this is my mind, and the rest of it is outside. There is no boundary to your mind; there is no place where your mind is not. There is no distance between you and me, although there is separation between you and me, and that separation is the greatest gift of all.

When we become involved in spiritual practices and spiritual ideas, we come to the idea that all is one and separation is bad. But that is childish. All is one, and separation is part of it. And without separation, we would not have this capacity to speak to each other. You are me, you are absolutely the same as me. And yet, I can speak to you, and look at you, and listen to you, because of the gift of the sense of separation.

Being born human, it is just incomprehensible that such a thing could be. It is already incomprehensible that anything could be in the first place. How can this be? How can it come about that there are people, and planets, and stars, and floors and ceilings, and flowers and rocks, and dirt? And, then, compounding the incomprehensible miracle of being itself, of existence itself, is this wonder of being human, of being in a human body, of being incarnate in a human mind, with all of the senses, and the reactions, and the responses, and the sensations and the relationships. This is unbelievable.

And, as a result of the long term mistake that we have made, the mistake that has been going on for thousands of years in human beings, we have come to believe that we are just this body, just this memory, this history, these thoughts, these sensations, these fears, these pains, these disappointments, these successes, these triumphs. And we seek, therefore, fearfully, to protect ourselves, to protect our view of things, to protect our bodies, to protect our relationships, and what we have. We want to hold our circumstance. We are fighting every moment, every breath, to protect, to hold, to be small, to be limited, to not suffer pain, to not be confronted with hardship, to not have wrong thoughts, or neurotic patterns of behavior. "I can't have that, I've got to do something about that." And it is unnecessary, really.

You are everything, you are all of it, and for me, in this life, this is all John. And I am so flooded with... I can't think of a word... I'd say *delight,* but it is not exactly a delight. It's the *fun* of it. The fun of being alive, the fun of facing death, the fun of facing the possibility of catastrophic loss, the fun of contending with whatever comes, or running from whatever comes, the fun of being stupid, the fun of being smart, the fun of being right, the fun of being wrong.

Nothing is at stake here. No one is harmed. No harm is caused, nothing is helped. What a gift that I should have this wondrous opportunity to be a self-aware human being.

Look and see if there is any boundary to your mind. Look and see. Check it out. See if you can find someplace where your mind ends. We have a local cluster of thoughts, and patterns of behavior, and conditioned responses, and so forth, that we think of as *our mind*. But, really, look beyond that. Does your mind not extend further than that? Sure, there is some reason for maintaining this sense of "This is me, and the rest of it is everything else", but it is a lie. There are not two human minds anywhere to be found.

The truth is that everything I see is me, and I can't find any place where this mind ends. I can find the local cluster, and I can deal with that, that is part of the fun. But I can't find any place where this mind ends. So, missing in this local cluster is this sense that I am this life, and that I am at stake in this life. That is gone in this local cluster. So, the gift is the wonder of the full participation in the life, the full welcoming and seeing the amazing, miraculous gift of being in the life. That is the result of having an end to that idea that I am this life. It seems counterintuitive, but it is the truth. It is my report. Rather than getting more distance from the life, I am totally immersed in the life. Why would I not be? Why would I want not to be?

This is not a separate mind, and if there plays within your mind the conviction that you are that life, that you are at stake in that life, that you have to be constantly attentive lest you do something wrong, lest you get hurt, or lest you hurt somebody else, if this idea of misery and suffering and isolation and contraction plays in that local cluster over there, then it plays in me. There is no protection here from that thought in your mind. There is no wall here where I can say, "Oh, I am free, you guys go about your business." The presence of the thought of bondage in any human mind is present in every human mind, in all of human consciousness.

The outcome of this, in all of the traditions, with the actual possible exception only of the neo-advaitists, who now are our special contribution to the spiritual life, is that the importance of compassion is huge. In fact, without compassion, in all of the traditions, there is nothing. The whole idea of liberation, without compassion, is foolishness. In Buddhism, at least in Tibetan Buddhism, it is so important that it becomes a fundamental practice, and there are meditation practices that are designed to produce the experience and the characteristic, the quality of compassion in the mind that undertakes them. In all of the traditions, without compassion, we have nothing.

The whole idea of individual liberation is a lie. It is a vicious lie. Without compassion there is nothing. And that is the reason why, in spiritual circles, the whole idea of being loving, and welcoming, and open-hearted, and generous and compassionate is so big, why the whole business about love is so big. It is because we know that. We know that there is nothing for me if you are bound.

So we try to get compassionate, that is part of our spiritual practice. As I said, in Tibetan Buddhism, there are very powerful meditation practices designed to engender compassion in the individual mind. So we try to get compassionate. I am not, and maybe not many of us here are, strict Tibetan Buddhists that have gone through Mahamudra and Tong Lin meditation, but we want to be compassionate. And we honor compassion. We honor those who obviously care about what happens to the rest of humanity. And we want to be like that ourselves. First, I might want to get rich, but even if I want to get rich first, still I have within me this underlying sense at least to pretend to be compassionate. And that doesn't work, either. If I am rich, I can give my money away, but that is not compassion.

The word "compassion" in English actually comes from Latin, through French. In English, the word compassion literally means "to suffer with". It doesn't mean to get all gooey-eyed and say, "Oh, let me help you, let me make everything better for you." Compassion is our nature. It means "to suffer with" because if the idea of bondage and suffering exists in any human being, it exists in *me*. Much of the work that we do to isolate ourselves and protect this local cluster is done in order to prevent *your* suffering and *your* misery from impinging on *my* little world, where I've got things pretty much together.

So, the inquiry leads inevitably to the realization that we are one, and that if *you* are bound, *I* am not free. The inquiry leads inevitably to a quality in the personality that grows bigger with time, a quality of wanting to see everybody rid themselves of this stupid lie. And this is what brings me to this line of work.

You can expect that you will be sensitive to the suffering of others, because the suffering of others is *your* suffering. You can expect that you will feel, maybe with much more intensity than you have in the past, the misery, aggression, and hatefulness of the people around you, because there is no refuge for you anywhere from yourself. But that too is immensely filled with fun and satisfaction. We have held it off for all of our lives, thinking that we will be harmed by it. But when the idea that we will be harmed by it is gone, that intimate experiencing of the misery and stupidity of all human beings is seen as a gift. It is part of the immense fun of being alive, of being incarnate, of being human. And the wonder of it is that it turns out there is actually something that we can do about it. That is the great good news. It is really fun when you can do something about it, and we can. We can encourage people to just tell the simple truth about what is happening with them.

The history of humanity, which is the history of me, is a horror story. We think that these times we are in now are really terrible, that the things that are being done by our government are criminal, and horrible, and the things that are being done by the terrorists and the things that are being done by people all over the world, the Blackwaters and the oil companies, and the destruction of the environment... But we are really pikers when it comes to inflicting horror.

We have been doing this for as long as we have been human. We have beheaded people by the thousands and made mountains of their skulls. We have burned witches, we have tortured people, and we have taken their lives. We have given in to every manner of hatred, and aggression, and rapaciousness, and horrifying behavior, all driven by one thing only: the belief that I am this life and nothing else. Every severed head, every stroke of the whip, every flicker of the flame that burns the saints at the cross, every bullet, every bit of it arises from this idea that I am nothing but this life, and I must protect myself at all cost. I must be right, I must be good, I must be true. And if you see things differently than me, you have got to go, because I can't keep my eye on you all the time.

I am filled with the sense of what is possible, if ten percent of human beings rid themselves of this false idea. Let's say, twenty percent. What would the world be like? It would be much different than it is now, I tell you that. We would play together. The drama itself would not need to be so vicious, I promise you that. It would be much different. And the greatness of this is that it is so easy, so simple. It doesn't take anything, really. It is so easy. How hard can it be?

So, that is the other side of it. You are absolutely alone in the inquiry. No one can help you there. No one can take you there. No one can show you yourself. And you are absolutely wide open and unprotected from the whole of human consciousness. You always have been, and now you see it. You always have been. That is why we protect ourselves so much. It is not just from our own false ideas, from our own stupidity; it is from the horror show that human minds are.

A couple of questions have come up in relation to what you are saying, that have to do with a sort of a challenge in my personal life. So, can I tell you, really briefly, the situation?

Sure.

First of all, I'm kind of new to what you are talking about.

That's good.

In a way, I am. I have two questions. First of all, we have two young daughters, one of whom is special needs, or I would call high maintenance. So, before the children, I spent years studying Krishnamurti, and looking into myself, and walking, and felt pretty solid. Then we adopted these two children, and they came with some issues of their own, so it has been really challenging, and rewarding, as well. But at times my husband and I felt like we were at the end of our rope in terms of being able to manage their demands 24/7, after being used to having more space in our life. A couple of years ago, that is where we were at, and then my husband was diagnosed with a rare cancer, and it has metastasized through his body, and that really added another level of challenge. So, that is the situation. He really wants to live. We are trying to find ways to keep him around, and we don't know the outcome. So it has been a fair amount of stress, a lot of surgeries, and it has been difficult for the children. I have a lot of fear about losing my husband. I don't want to. I have a lot of fear about the possibility that he is going to die a lot sooner than I would have hoped.

Yes, of course you do.

And I feel like I have done enough looking to know that if I do need to lose him, if he does need to die, I could handle that, I could just go on retreat, and just look, and just be with that, until I took it in. I feel like I would be okay. But I have these two little girls now, and I am not going to have the option of a retreat. So I have a lot of fear about how I am going to deal with this if it happens, and I know it is in the future, but it just keeps coming up, and I

*am afraid I am going to have two brokenhearted little girls, and I
don't know how I am going to be able to stay in touch with who I
am, and bring some equanimity to that situation. And I guess the
other part of the question is, What about helping young children
who are already caught in the belief that they are their life?*

The only thing you can do is tell the truth. Not to tell them,
"Okay, you have to do this, and you have to learn who you really
are." But just, when confronted with a need for a response, always
tell the truth. That is the best thing anybody can do for children,
always tell the truth. And if you haven't been telling the truth, you
just start telling the truth. No matter what it is, if you respond
with the truth, everything will be okay.

As to the horrible circumstance that you face, the possible
loss of your husband, and even without the loss of your husband,
this fight against cancer is a horrifying thing. It is hard. It is
frightening, and it is unfair. There is no justice to it. Most spiritual
teachers, I think, would tell you that the only thing you can do is
to not resist any of it, not resist the fear, not resist the expectation,
not resist your own inability to handle it, not resist anything, to
receive everything as it comes, and it will come and it will go.

But I tell you, I don't know any way that you can stop resisting,
because the resistance is part of this personality. It is part of this
character, it is part of its qualities, and is part of the qualities of
everybody. If Carla were to die, there would be huge resistance
arising in me to the consequences of that. And there would be
nothing whatsoever that I could do about that. No matter who
preaches to you and tells you, "Don't resist," you can say to them,
"Tell me how." And I'll tell you how. "How" is to begin and stay
with the inquiry until every last vestige of this belief that you are
at stake in this life is gone. And with it will go the resistance. It
is not going to make things good, but the resistance to them will
be unavailable to you. And then, however things unfold, you are
totally receiving them; and if you totally receive them, when they

go, they are gone. They can't hurt you. Death can't hurt you. But the only way to know that is to be finished with resistance, and the only way to be finished with resistance is to be finished with this absolutely unseen and unconscious belief that you are this life. And the only way to do that, in my experience, is to look directly at the reality of what you are, as often as you can.

This weekend, we actually have some space; we have a lot of friends helping us out, so that we can come here, which we really appreciate. And there is actually no resistance this weekend. The situation is the same, but we have the space this weekend, and we are inquiring together, and it feels very rich. So I really value that. But mostly, the day-to-day life, with the kids and all, it doesn't feel too spacious.

No, it doesn't feel too spacious, and it is not. But you are. The gift of this retreat concerning yourself with self-inquiry is huge. But what it does is it gets you started. That is the usefulness of it. There is no finishing of you. It gets you started, it puts you in an environment and in an atmosphere where resistance can safely be discarded for this time, and you can safely engage in this practice. When you leave the retreat and go back to your life with the problematic children, and the husband dying of cancer, as you are finishing up this retreat, notice, as you are doing the inquiry, how little it takes. It really takes very little, just a moment.

I advise everybody to go ahead, sit down, quiet your mind and get a sense of what it really is to look at the truth of what you are, the reality of what you are, and then, when you go back to the world, where things are constantly assailing you, then you will know in your heart that it is really easy to do this inquiry in the midst of all of it. It only takes a minute. Doing the dishes, sweeping the floor, any activity, anything you are doing is grist for the mill of self-inquiry, because there are always these two components: there are all the things that are happening, and there is you.

And in the midst of anything, you can find a time, a moment, to just stop for a second and check and see if you are not still here, and if you have been touched by any of it. Because the point of doing that is not to persuade you that you are still here and you are not touched by it, but just to give you an idea of where to look, because it is the looking that does it.

Are you saying it is not necessary to have a lot of time to engage in it?

That's right, you don't need a lot of time.

That's a good thing.

You are going to sleep at night, you have a couple of minutes then, you wake up in the morning, you have a couple of minutes then. You are in the bathroom, brushing your teeth, you have a couple of minutes then…

I appreciate your teaching, particularly right now, because it is fairly simple, and I don't have to be thinking of all the different ways I might approach myself that I don't have time to do. I don't have time to read all the books anymore, and I don't have time to take long walks…

It is simple. That's right. That's a good thing.

It's nice to just have a simple instruction, "Just look."

Yes, it's very simple. Let me know. Stay in touch with me.

Thanks, I appreciate that.

And if you ever need to speak with me, you can make arrangements and we can talk on the phone. That's true for all of you. You can write to me, you can come to the online meetings. If you live in Ojai or Santa Monica, you can come to a meeting. If you need to talk to me about something that is really critical for you, you can make arrangements so that we can talk on the phone. I am your servant, really. That is my job, to be your servant.

Okay. Thank you.

I am happy you are here.

Thank you, I am, too.

Okay, we are going to have to stop now. Well, what can I say? Except thank you again, and I will see you this afternoon. I have some things that I really want to convey to you, like I did this morning, but then I want to hear from you. So I probably won't have too much to say this afternoon, although you never know with me... *(laughter)* Thank you so much for this time. I am in love with this retreat. I think this is really good for the world.

Meeting 5

November 4, 2007 - Afternoon

Good evening. Welcome back. I am happy to be here with you. Does anybody have anything to say?

I wanted to let you know that in all of my years of seeking, I had never resonated with self-inquiry. I had been aware of it, but I had never really resonated with it, until I met you in Arizona. It was miraculous how I met you. I won't go into it, but, in any event, you inspired me to embark on the process of self-inquiry. As a result of that process, there have been two seemingly distinctive experiences, and I am curious about the distinction between the two. The first experience is one of hereness and awareness of this body, and what is in the environment, and it is somewhat localized. But then, sometimes, subsequent to that, there is a collapsing back into another level, I guess you could say, where it feels like crystal-clear, pure consciousness, with no frame of reference whatsoever, and very natural and really simple. Of course, it only feels like that in retrospect, because nothing is going on during the experience itself; it's only when the me comes back, and I review it. What are the mechanics, why does that transition happen? What is that transition? Why are there these two different experiences?

This crystal-clear consciousness without a frame of reference, is this new?

No, but it has happened more frequently.

Yes, but that is not what I mean. I don't mean it as: 'Has it happened more than once?' Is it something that you don't recognize? Is it something brand-new to you?

No, it's very intimate.

It is permanent, right? I mean, it is here.

Right.

That is you.

But it is not here…

The inquiry itself is taking place within the lie that you are this life and, therefore, you are at stake here, so that the actual apperception seems to be of something separate and apart from you. When you see yourself from within the lie, it feels like you are seeing something else. The way to test this is to determine whether what you are seeing is something that has never been here before, or something that has always been here and you just hadn't noticed that you are always seeing it.

The other experiences, the kind of body-based experiences, these are just experiences. I mean, they are just body sensations, emotional sensations, things of that nature. The feeling of 'I am' is an experience; it is a definite, energetic, sensational experience. It is not reality, it comes and goes. It comes with the 'I' and it goes with the 'I', and you are not aware of it at all times. It is the same with the rest of the stuff you are referring to. These are sensational experiences that are just in the nature of the way the body energy works. We can make a lot out of them, but I prefer not to.

That experience of no frame of reference, and the perception of that which has no basis for saying anything about itself, that clarity and simplicity, that is you, and that is always here. Now, the place where we may go wrong in the inquiry is to imagine that the purpose of the inquiry is to make the consciousness of that reality ever-present, so that it displaces everything else, the problematic things and the nuts and bolts of living. Because that is what we have been kind of conditioned to do in the spiritual realm, we have been conditioned to look for some new state, some new, transcendental reality that will displace everything else, and make everything else go away.

So it is important to see that the goal of the inquiry is not that. This reality is always here. It is never absent, it is never gone. Sometimes you notice it, sometimes you don't notice it. But the point of the inquiry is to deliberately notice it. It is to *deliberately* look at it from within this lie, not for any purpose other than to let the light in. And the light disintegrates this belief that you are whatever the belief says you are.

So, this is what makes it difficult to speak about the inquiry, because we are so accustomed to thinking that our spiritual practices are intended to produce some transcendental state, some final transcendence, or something of that nature. We are not accustomed to thinking of them in practical terms where they are just something we do to cure ourselves of a disease.

The natural state is the state of the conscious, ever-present awareness of reality. That is your natural state. It is the natural state of human beings. It is this consciousness, this self-aware consciousness of what you are. That is the outcome of the inquiry: the natural state asserts itself, and stabilizes itself. It is not that some new state takes over. So, is that helpful? Did that answer your question?

Parts of it did. But it also kind of brings up a little bit of confusion.

It seems like everything I say does that. A little bit of clarity, a little bit of confusion. *(laughter)*

So, are you saying that the phenomenon of transcendence is potentially a hindrance to understanding, too?

The seeking after the phenomenon of transcendence is certainly a hindrance, because it is a wrong turn. I mean a hindrance in the sense that it is wasting time, if what you want is to be finished with searching for the transcendental experience, searching for a solution to the life, a solution to the difficulty of life. If that is what you want, then believing yourself to be seeking after a transcendental experience in service to that is a waste of time. There is nothing wrong with seeking a transcendental experience, if you see it for what it is. You can even get it with drugs. There is nothing wrong with transcendental experiences; there is nothing wrong with seeking them. It just has nothing to do with the realm of self-inquiry. Self-inquiry has bigger game than a passing experience, no matter how wonderful it might be.

Do you have any recommendations to help inspire a different direction, then? I am not sure how to phrase the question. I guess it is just to look at yourself, and not worry about it...

That's it. And don't worry about getting sidetracked, either. That is just the nature of this apparatus that makes up the personality and its qualities and characteristics. There is not anything you can do about it. You get sidetracked, and then you remember, and then you come back. The essential instruction is to do it whenever it occurs to you to do it. The fact that it occurs to you to do it is the appearance of this conscious intent to see what is true. So, whenever it occurs to you to do it, do so. Look at yourself. See if you can't get a glimpse of this silent presence that you are. The point of that is not to understand this presence, or to make it into something, but just to look at it. That is why I keep saying that all the work is in the looking. That is all there is. The looking does the work, whenever you can, whenever you think of it.

Thank you. That's very clear.

There is something about this practice that can seem kind of confusing because, on the one hand I say, "You've got to do this if you really want to be free of misery and suffering in your life, this is what you have to do, you have to look at yourself. Right now. Look at yourself." And on the other hand, I say, "Well, don't worry about it if you are not looking at yourself, because you will. It will occur to you, and you will come back to it." But that is the way it is, that is why it is for adults. It is not like it is some strict regimen in which you have to follow certain specific times and postures, and things of that nature. It is for adults. It is the recognition that my desire is to see the reality of what I am, the actuality of what I am, and implementing that using all of your own native intelligence and common sense. No one can tell you how, really. I can tell you to do it whenever you can. I can hear your reports, and recognize from my own experience that what you are seeing is real, but I can't tell you how to do it. It is for adults, it is for self-actualizing adults, if you will.

It's wonderful to be here. I was really moved by the previous session, and I have some questions. You said to look to see if there were any boundaries to the mind, and that confused me, because I find that when I look at myself, the mind sort of stands at the door, I don't bring the mind there.

Says who? How could the mind be separate from self? It is the mind that is looking for itself.

Well, then I am confused about what the mind is, because the thinking part of my mind doesn't go there.

Everybody is confused about what the mind is. Nobody knows what the mind is. And that's because it is boundary-less. Nobody knows *what* it is. If you try to find someplace where it ends, well, good luck with that.

Well, is there then no difference between the mind and self?

Actually, no, there isn't. What is the mind, what is it made up of? What is its substance? Waves are made of water, right? Clouds are made of water, too. Mind is made of self, which is a word that I don't usually use in this context, because it is so fraught with everybody else's understanding of what it is. But mind is made of self, mind is made of you. Everything is made of you. There is nothing to be found anywhere that doesn't have as its essential component, you.

Which is sort of my other question. I guess I don't experience that. I know it, and I believe it, but I don't experience that.

Actually, you do experience that, but you don't recognize what you experience as being the experience of that. The fact is that we always, forever, only experience that essential inseparability, indissolubility of reality that is the nature of things everywhere. There is never a moment when we are not experiencing that. What we don't experience is the understanding of that, or what we imagine should be the way it feels, right?

I think there is a big expectation.

Right, but we are always experiencing that; that is the truth. And when we have been in spiritual pursuits for a long time, even those of us who are well along the road in the inquiry, we form these deep-seated, unseen ideas of what reality should be. We don't even verbalize those ideas; we just have this deep-seated sense of what reality ought to feel like. And it doesn't feel like that, it feels just like you. It feels just like you do now, right now, just exactly like that. That is what reality feels like, that is what the absolute feels like: just like you feel, right now, exactly like that.

So, we think that since we are not coming upon some new breakthrough in clarity and understanding, we don't see this. But I say, you always see this, you just don't know you do; you just think you are looking at something else. You think you are looking at separation, when you are actually looking at unity. Go figure.

But some people seem to express very consciously the feeling of unity, which leads me to think, "Well, I also should sense that, too."

You mean, like Rumi, and people like that?

People who speak here, about the sense of me being you...

But see, that is not what the truth is. The truth is that everything is you. That is the truth. The truth is that there is nothing to be found anywhere but you. It is not like there is me and you, and we are the same. It is just you. That is all there is, just you. There is no me, there is just you...

Then why don't I know that?

But you do. You do know that. These are just thoughts about it, and you pay more attention to the thoughts about what it should be than you do to the actuality of what you know. Knowing is really simple, it is not complicated. Our thoughts and our stories about it, they get very complicated, very subtle, and very nuanced; but reality is very simple, the knowing is very simple. It has no content to it, for one thing. It has no content to it, no storyline to it; it is just the silent knowing. And that is always here, it is never absent. It is the same as you, it is you. We are trying with all of our hearts to see what we are always already seeing, and we are trying with all of our hearts to know what we are always already knowing. That is our nature, the seeing and knowing; there is nothing more to us than that. So, I say that you see exactly as I do, and you say, "Oh, no, I don't, because of this and that and the other thing…"

Just relax…

Just keep up the inquiry. These things take time. It takes time for the false to disintegrate. It takes time for you to notice that has happened. It takes time for it to dawn on you that there is no strife in your life, even though there is hardship or pain, and that the engine of antagonistic internal warfare is quiet. It takes time for you to notice those things. And it takes time for you to notice the fact that you have always seen reality, that it is not something that you can attain. The reason it is not something you can attain is because the thing that we are trying to attain is what we are. So, just keep up the inquiry. That is the only thing to do. Ramana once said to somebody, "The day will come when you will laugh, and that day is exactly the same as this day."

Okay. Thank you. (laughing)

See? There you are, laughing already.

Hello.

Hi, I'm the husband dying of cancer.

You are the guy dying of cancer?

As introduced.

Well, I am happy to meet you before that happens.

So I guess my question has to do with the role of the body in this self-inquiry. Being given such a diagnosis has quickened the...

Yes, it does tend to concentrate the mind, as they say.

Facing your mortality, being intelligent about doing what you can do, and letting go of what you can't have a say over. There is now obviously a desire to continue to live, even just to see how things work out, just to watch my girls grow up, or see if we can get out of these crazy messes we have gotten into in the world. Just to stay in the game, just to be around, it seems to take a body, and I have got one, and I don't know about the afterlife and all that... Not being sure if anything that I am doing is contributing to facilitating healing, or furthering the growth of the cancer cells, whatever things I might do in the day, there is sort of a shadow cast over that, since I don't know, and it is hard to not be invested in the outcome. In a sense, I am not too attached to my personality, that can go. But my body... It is confusing to face the loss of that. So I just wondered if you could shed some light on that.

Who would be the one that suffered the loss?

I'm here. I get that.

Yes, you are.

But I seem to need a body to be here, and that is what I am not sure about. Do I?

Here's the thing. Inquiry will not answer that question. It won't. What inquiry will do is rid you of the belief that you are the body. Inquiry will not remove from you the fear and trembling at the prospect of the death of the body. What it will do is remove from you the belief that you are the body. That it will do. This body, this mind, these senses, this intelligence, this is all a tool that you use. It is an instrument that you use to perceive yourself in the world, in everything there is. All of these bodies are that to you.

You may beat the cancer, and I hope you do, but when this body goes, so too goes the personal consciousness, the entity that seems so real. It goes, it is just gone. But the terror of losing the body, the terror of dying belongs entirely to this entity that will die, and will be unable to lament having left, that is the truth of it.

And that is the truth, no matter whether the cancer kills you in a week, or life just finally departs from you in fifty years. However this transpires, you have the time now to settle one thing, finally, once and for all, beyond all possibility of confusion. And that is, what is your actual nature? What are you really? If you are the body, then you can know that; if you are that in which the body comes and goes, then you can know that also. That is absolutely your birthright, and it is absolutely possible, in whatever time remains in this life, for you and for all the rest of us. What is not possible is to stop this body, and this person, from dying. It may be possible to beat the cancer, and fight it all you can, but in the end, it is going to go. The opportunity now is, again, to find out what you are; to know, beyond a shadow of a doubt, what you are. And that I can offer you.

I can't offer you answers as to the afterlife or things like that, because so far as I can tell, when the body goes, personal consciousness goes with it. And that is actually a good thing, since there is no personal consciousness left to lament having left. But see what you are. During this period of fighting this disease, when it occurs to you to do so, use this time to destroy the real, fundamental disease, which is the belief that you are this life. That you can do. Do you follow me?

Yes.

I am very happy to meet you. Will you stay in touch with me?

Yes.

I am very happy to be here again, and I appreciate you to no end. Sometimes, during the practice of looking at myself, I wonder about the progression, and I look for it in the things you have said, and I don't always get it. There is remembering... When I remember, sometimes it's a lot, sometimes it's the whole day, or almost a day, if I am very busy. I wondered what your experience was over time, when you were sitting on your bed and you were looking, and then you saw what you were looking for, and then you remember when you can remember, or when it happens to happen. And it seems like in my mind there is a gap of maybe what to expect and what happened with you, what your experience is. Sometimes there is like a background knowing, but sometimes it is not there, and I thought it would be helpful to have a little more insight into what happens over time. Is that valuable? It seems to me it would be.

What happens as a consequence of the inquiry over time?

Yes, and how it progresses. How it has progressed with you as far as remembering to look. Is there an effort? Is there still a time when you don't remember, and then you do remember? Does the looking become just part of who you are, and you don't need to remember, because you are always seeing this?

The truth of the matter is this: always, you are seeing reality. I know I might sound like a broken record, but it is really hard to get this across. Always you are seeing reality. As you sit there right now, asking me this question about how things progress, and does there come a time when you don't need to remember to look, you are absolutely seeing reality. There is nothing whatsoever that is obscuring your vision of reality, of what you are. There is no need for you ever to remember to look at yourself, because you are always seeing yourself. The only thing that produces the need to remember to look at yourself is the persistence of this underlying belief that you are whatever you believe yourself to be, and you don't even know what you believe yourself to be. So that, as long as it seems to you that you need to remember to consciously look to see what it feels like to be, for as long as that is the case, then that is an indication that the shreds, the last die-hard remnants of this belief are still present and operating unbeknownst to you.

It is also true that that may not be so. But it doesn't matter if it is not so, because it seems to be so. What I mean by that is that the belief is usually gone before you really notice it is gone. There is really no problem, but we have, for the sake of this effort, agreed to define a belief about what you are as the problem. That problem vanishes while you are still trying to get rid of it. That is the truth. It vanishes as the result of having the light fall upon it, or the medicine do its work, or whatever metaphor strikes your fancy. It vanishes as a result of the inquiry proceeding as it does. It may be some time before you realize that there is no problem. As long as it seems to you necessary to consciously and deliberately and with intent look to see that you are as you are, do so.

Even before it is gone, you are already what you are trying to be. Even when the inquiry first begins, it is beginning within you, who are already what you are trying to become. So, keep it going until you don't think about it anymore, until there doesn't seem to be any sticky suffering to you.

Sometimes, I have the feeling I know that I am here and I don't need to remember.

That's right.

And so I don't. I am aware of me being here. Well, there is this background knowing that I am here, and sometimes that is not there.

Well, it is, but you don't notice it.

Sometimes I am not consciously aware that that is there, and it seems like it is not there. And then I remember, when I remember.

Is there in you a constant murmur of anxiety?

I don't think so. That seems to be changing.

That seems to be gone to me, when I see you over these years that we have been in this relationship. That is the sign that the inquiry is doing its job. That constant, underlying quiet murmur of anxiety, "Am I doing this right?", when that goes, you are pretty much home free.

I used to have the feeling that I was missing something, and then there was this yearning. But that is gone. Occasionally, I am concerned about that. Occasionally, I think that if I don't have that, there is nothing. I mean, that goes with that knowing.

That is what you were afraid you were missing all these years, this that is always here. It always comes back to the same thing: whenever it occurs to you to do so, do so. It is the occurring to you that should be followed, that should be honored; if it occurs to you to do it, do it.

So simple. Thank you.

It is really simple. As I said, it is for adults, because we don't make up charts and diagrams and say, "Okay, at ten o'clock in the morning you sit down and do this, and at one o'clock in the afternoon you sit down and do this, and so forth." It is just whenever it occurs to you to look at yourself, look at yourself. And everything else will be taken care of.

∞

What a pleasure to see you, my friend.

It is very special to be here, John. I just wanted to ask you about something that I experience all the time. It is part of my nature to plan ahead and to think about things that are to come in the future, and it takes away from being spontaneous, and being alive.

Do you think so? You must have a different experience of things than I do. I have never found anything that isn't entirely spontaneous.

Well, they are spontaneous, you bet.

Of course they are, in the moment...

But they are also distractions. And especially, I don't know if it is because I want to control something, or I am afraid of something...

That is a different story. Now you are talking about motivation rather than talking about just the apparatus operating. The apparatus operating is always entirely spontaneous, it just arises. The planning arises, the fulfillment of the plans, or the failure to fulfill them, that arises, too. But the idea that the planning is going to save you from anxiety and fearfulness about losing control, that is just misery and suffering. And that only can arise because of the deep-seated, unseen belief that you are at stake in this life.

It only makes it worse.

What does? The planning?

The planning that isn't necessary.

I don't think you can do anything about the planning. I don't think you can do anything about it. Consider this. This is what we have done for all these thousands of years: we have tried to figure out how to make ourselves, our personalities, our minds clean and clear and pure and unsullied by false motives. That never has worked. We think, "Well, the problem is that I am making these plans in order to protect myself against the loss of control, so what I have to do is to stop making these plans." But I don't think you are going to succeed at that because, so far as I can tell, you don't have anything to say about that part of it anyway.

I don't have to pay attention to them.

No, you don't. You don't have to pay attention to anything that is occurring, any of the ways in which life is living itself. You can, right? It is not going to hurt you to do so, but it is not going to hurt you to not do so, either. The only thing you can do that can help is to look at yourself.

It feels right to me to just look at myself and let this stuff go.

That's right. There is nothing you can do anyway. We talk about letting things go, but how can you hold onto anything? How do you do that? What is the secret? It sounds like magic, right? You look at yourself. The thing that plagues you is this underlying sense that you are going to lose control and that control is really important because, after all, you are at stake in this life. If you don't get it right, god knows what will happen. The solution to that is not to try and persuade yourself that it is not true, either by paying attention to what I say, or reading spiritual books, for example. The solution to that is to expose the lie to reality by looking at yourself. And then you can fight with making plans, or not fight with making plans. You can make plans, you can not make plans; you can hate the fact that you make plans, or you can love the fact that you make plans. Who cares? Who is hurt? Do you see?

Yes, I see. Thank you.

You are very welcome. It's good to see you.

It's really good to be here.

This whole business of doing the right thing and making sure that what we do is the right thing, even if what we are trying to do is to stop trying to control, or stop trying to make rules, it just overlooks our everyday life experience, which should teach us that we don't have anything to say about what happens in these lives. By the time anything happens, by the time we notice it, it has already happened. By the time we notice a thought, it is already here. Who can decide to think anything in particular? And yet, despite our continuous life experience to this effect, we continue to torture and torment ourselves by trying to do something about these things that just happen.

☙

This is the first time I am here. I am glad to be here. I want to reflect a little bit that it is like the game "You're it!" I am grateful to be human, because all the wonderful things that come up, creative mind, all the challenges and everything, it's just part of who I am. And one of the things I realize in this process is that I have a tendency to internalize the external, and that seems to be the biggest part of the lie. And it doesn't mean that the external is not happening, but just looking in, it seems to let everything go. Just this looking, and not attaching to what I am looking for, and just trying to find the source, and there is a sense of calmness in that looking...

Yes, that is a sign.

I just wanted to share that with you.

That is very good news. That is a common report. The looking in produces a sense of calm, and if you keep it up, you will be really surprised.

Well, I'm surprised already. Thank you.

You are very welcome. I think we are going to have to stop now, as much as I hate to leave you, guys. I really do, you know? It is really hard. Please, reflect on the things we have talked about today. But above all else, see if you cannot manage to try to look at yourself. Try to look at reality. Try to have the conscious awareness of this awareness that is always here. All I want is for you to try, to start. Then, everything else will be taken care of. Okay? Sleep well, or, if you don't sleep well, make good use of the time, and I will see you in the morning. I will see some of you in a little while, but I will see everybody in the morning. I am really grateful to be here with you. I am really grateful for your presence here, and your attention, and your time. I am at your service.

Meeting 6

November 5, 2007 - Morning

Good morning, welcome. Here we are again. Does anybody have anything to say?

Last night I remembered a statement that I read in a Ramana book about a little girl who was living at Arunachala Ashram. They were talking about best friends. Everybody was talking about who their best friend was, and she was asked, and she said Dr. So-and-So was her best friend. And then they said, "How come you didn't say Ramana?" And she said, "He's everything, he is everywhere." And then they said, "But don't you see him in the body, don't you see him sitting, don't you feel his touch, don't you follow him walking?" And at that point, she said, "I'm going to stop talking now." I never not see Ramana and Arunachala as anything but everything. I experience that, always. And if I ask myself, What is that? Is that my teacher? It's never that. You are never separate from Carla. You and Carla come together; you have always been together in my head, before I even met you, you and Carla were together. I can't separate you.

That is very discerning of you.

I didn't know you, and yet you were Carla and John, John and Carla. And Ramana. First, Ramana. And my connection was to offer you a painting of Ramana. And now it is never separate from Ramana and Arunachala, and you. But you and Carla, it's not life, it comes to me as friends...

Friends.

And everything has a voice. There isn't anything in my life that doesn't direct me, as I allow it to. It is always present. Even a piece of paper has a voice. Like you said, the rocks were singing to you. But I am always present. There is always a me-identification, no matter what I see.

Wait, wait, wait, wait…

It's not a like I am that piece of paper…

So?

Well, you spoke last night about the loss of… That you are all there is… And yet, I see all as part of me…

You are all. There is nothing but you anywhere to be found, including the experience of me, including the experience of separation, including the experience of the paper, of the paper having a voice. That is all you. The whole thing is you. It is not like there is no differentiation in reality. It is all you, including the differentiation, including the relationship, including the feeling of separation, including even feelings of isolation, and lostness. All of that is you. The whole show is you. The mistake we make when we try to understand the transmission that all is one, that there is only one, or not-two, is we think we know what that means, what it is pointing to. But what it is pointing to is things just as they are, not things differently seen or differently felt. Things, just as they are, are of one essence, and that essence is you. That is what I mean. If you take out the tears and the friendship, and the animosity, and the antagonism, and all that, where is the fun? *(laughter)*

So, what I am saying is that just exactly as you see things, that is exactly as things are. Exactly. And there is only one. Less than one, there is only you. And you already see things like that, you just don't recognize that you see things like that. And that is what, of course, leads us to a lot of spiritual suffering, because we have this idea of how the realized ones perceive the world, or how I would perceive the world if I saw all as one. And we try to get that, which is absurd. Ramana insisted that the only thing standing between you and self-realization is the belief that you are not already realized just as you are; that your vision of things is the vision of realization, just as it is. Nothing needs to be changed about that, nothing.

God knows we haven't had any luck in doing anything about that. I am not so interested in talking about the wonder and the magnificence of all is one. The only thing that really interests me is what it takes to destroy whatever it is that is present in you that makes you think that you need something that you don't have; that there is something to see that you are not seeing, and that you are at stake in this life. That is all that needs to go. And the one activity that, in my experience, is the final act, and brings about the end of the search, is the exposing of this apparatus to the reality of its nature, by looking at yourself.

Well, it's exactly that. Because there is no way I have been able to not see me in any form I have ever appeared in.

There it is.

It's like that bunch of roses... There I am. I am not this all the time, this body, this color, this human, but it's always me...

That's right. And you see, it is always you, always.

Always me.

The reason you can't get away from that is because there is no place you can go to get away from you.

113

Yes, and it's amazing to me.

And that is the good news.

And there are people who say, "Oh, that's me, and I am that elephant, I am that mountain, I am that tree, I am that ugly man, I am that that..."

I have taken LSD in my youth, and I had much more bizarre experiences than that. *(laughter)* But here we are. We really torture ourselves, trying to imagine what we should be seeing, how it should look to us, how we should be feeling about things. You are just as you are, my sweet, just as you are.

Well, there didn't seem to be any conflict, until I kept hearing you say that somehow I wouldn't see a "me" whatever situation came about.

Did anybody else hear me say that? I can't believe I said that. If I said that, I should be shot. *(laughter)*

Well, I knew that it was my hearing. Cool.

Okay. You are so beautiful.

Thank you.

That is the whole game, really. It is the recognition, the insight, the possibility that just as we are is what we are trying to be. And we don't see that. We are trying desperately to be just exactly as we are. Why can't I get it? Why can't I be just as I am?

I'm here...

Yes, you are.

And it's amazing to me that I ever thought I wasn't.

It is, isn't it? What could you have been thinking?

What could I have been thinking? Yes, that is true. It's just amazing. This morning, I was just walking back and forth, up and down a path... And you know how sometimes they say that before you drop the body your whole life flashes before you?

Yes.

I had that experience this morning, all the spiritual experiences I have ever had, my whole life flashed in front of me, starting from when I was little girl, and my father had just died, and I was bereft and I thought Jesus was talking to me, and I felt I heard the sweetness and the love, and the comfort. And then, later on, the ascended masters were talking to me, and then the Buddha was talking to me, and Christ was talking to me... And one of the things I noticed in this experience was that there was one thing that was consistent, but that I had missed in all of these experiences, and that was that I was there.

Yes, that's right. That's the one thing we miss. That's excellent.

This is really funny, because it is so obvious. I have been doing the work I do for many years, and I have had so many clients and students that have been channelers, and healers, and psychics... And whenever they come to me, it is so clear to me that whatever they think is out there and is coming through them, is really them.

115

Yes. That is really amazing.

It's so clear to me. That's why they came to me. But do you think I could see it?

No. Go figure.

And I remember being woken up at four in the morning thinking some ascended master was talking to me, and I am writing down all this beautiful stuff... Never, ever, did it occur to me that they were in me. That they were me.

It's amazing.

I think I really fought knowing that. I wanted them to be out there somewhere, where I could adore them, and love them, and seek solace from them. I think I wanted to escape this world. I wanted to live somewhere that I thought was out there, rather than here.

We all do, really. The spiritual seekers among us, we all do. We imagine that the problem is this world, or the problem is this life, or the problem is my wrongheadedness, or the problem is that I can't get what I want, or the problem is that I do get what I want. And the thing that this points to, and that we also often don't see, is that the fact that we are always looking for a solution means that we know there is a problem. And no matter how hard we try, the solutions that we try to adopt don't fix the problem. But our sense is that the problem is embodiment, this life, this world, and that the solution, therefore, is outside this life, outside this world, somewhere else, in somebody else's life, in somebody else's utterances. Until we don't anymore, until we grow up.

That has fallen away, John. It is not there anymore.

Yes, it has. The inquiry takes that away, it really does.

And it is so interesting, because it feels like the inquiry is just beginning.

Yes.

Because I started out feeling like there were boundaries of what I thought was me...

That's right.

Amber has this song that has this line in it like "Boundaries are crashing, I've never noticed this before..." It doesn't feel like they are crashing, it just seems like they never were really there...

That's right, and you are just noticing they never were really there. That's right. When we make up spiritual songs, we have to be dramatic, otherwise it doesn't work. When we write poetry and sutras and shastras and hymns, we have got to make them juicy, otherwise it doesn't work. How can you sing a hymn to "Oh, I thought that was there, but it isn't!"? *(laughter)*

I wanted to talk to you a little bit about your talk yesterday morning, what you said about one mind, and that we couldn't go home, we couldn't really be free until all of that mind is free everywhere. And, I have this experience of oneness, with myself standing back and observing it, but then I noticed something else. When I looked for who was observing, there was no one there. And when you were talking about that yesterday, I couldn't stop crying, and every time I thought about it during the day, the tears would come again. I absolutely know that to be true.

Yes, it is true, and it is obvious. You know, once you see it, it is obvious. It's like the boundaries. Once you see it, it is obvious. And the seeing of that is compassion. Compassion is not an emotion, or action, or something like "Oh, you poor thing," or any of that. Compassion is seeing that we are all in this together. It is absolutely a fact that the only way to do the inquiry, the only way to see what is real, is on your own. Nobody can take you there. It is also absolutely a fact that we are all in this together. We sink or swim together, and that is obvious really in the world at large, in the material world.

Look at us. In Venezuela yesterday they had an ice and hail storm that was so bizarre that it filled the streets, and froze instantly into a river of ice, and trapped people in it. Look at us, look what we are doing. What have we done? And that is merely in the material world. In reality, we are just as much in this together; we are just as much at the mercy of each other, we are just as much one: one mind, one heart, one self.

It is so vital that we all know the truth.

Well, it is the only thing that is going to save us.

Yes, that is the only thing that is going to save us.

And we may not be saved, you know? That is possible, too. Who knows? But I know this: the only thing that will save us is to come face-to-face with reality. I know that. It is to rid ourselves of this infantile idiocy that has us contending against each other for what we imagine to be scarce spoils; that has us contending against each other for love, comfort, satisfaction, and that has us contending internally even with ourselves to make sure that we are doing right, to make sure that we are not doing wrong, to make sure that we are thinking the right things. All that can save us is the truth.

That's all I had to say.

That is plenty. I am so happy to see you. You know, you wander away, and I wonder what happened to you...

I never go anywhere.

I know that.

I love you, John.

Likewise.

Thank you.

You are welcome. Yes, it is crazy. We are nuts. The planet is trying to get rid of us. Anybody else?

∞

Just in the nick of time. I was just about to launch into a tirade...

Nice to see you. It is really fun to be here, in a certain way. And in a certain way, it isn't. Both are true. Isn't it interesting?

If it is all fun, then I am not doing my job...

Several people that I am very closely interfaced with, and in particular one person that I see intermittently, are in an incredible amount of pain. And, as you said, when we are in the presence of whatever it is, it becomes us to some degree or other...

Well, it is you. I don't say it becomes anything, it is you.

It is, but then, somewhere else, I am different. And then I go there, and it seems that certain patterns that I encounter are more familiar than others in human beings. In other words, they resonate with patterns within this personality, so it is even more excruciating. One of the people who is in a lot of pain is my son, and it is psychological pain, not physical pain. What do I do?

Tell the truth. Really, there is nothing else to do. And by that I don't mean preach to your son, but just when you are in communication and conversation of whatever sort with your son, tell the truth. Obviously, I don't know what the actual, specific, mechanical details of the psychological distress might be, but I know that if it is psychological, the source of the distress is always the same.

He hates people; he doesn't want to be alive. "Why was I born?" My boyfriend also feels this way, "I'm done."

How does that make you feel?

You know what? It pisses me off!

I don't blame you.

It's like, "Wake up, for god's sake!" It pisses me off! And then I want to engage with them, but when I engage, what is evoked, rather than presence and sinking into that, is anger.

It is a dance.

Yes, a dance, which I think they like.

Of course, they do.

I think they enjoy that.

Of course, they do.

To engage with it is fun, maybe, on some level.

The only thing you can do is tell the truth, and if they want to be free of this pain, the only thing they can do is find the truth. That's all. That is the end of the story. Now, you will engage with them. That is going to continue happening, that dance will continue playing out, and there is nothing you can say about that. But whenever you get the chance, tell them the truth, whatever the truth is; the simple truth, not complicated, not explaining everything, and wrapping everything up in a nice, neat understanding, a gestalt, but just the simple truth.

What comes to mind, frankly, is that I have to be the truth.

Well, you are the truth.

Consciously, rather than engaged in my mind, because then the tendency is to want to withdraw.

That's right, withdraw or engage, that is the same, it is two sides of the same. It is a protective strategy. What happens when we get involved in stories like that, at least this is my experience and what I suspect to be the case, is that we get engaged in stories of worthlessness and self-hatred, and hatred of the world, and all of that. One of the things that we are afraid of is that it might be true, that there might be a real basis for that. So our inclination, when relating from this belief that I am my life and that I am at stake in my life, our inclination is to try to prove that is not so, that there is no reason for you to feel that way. Of course, life is worth living, of course you are stupid to think it is not, right? All this is only serving two purposes. It is serving the purpose of the afflicted one, who wants to have that dance go on, and the purpose of the other afflicted one, which of course is you. It is serving the purpose of maintaining the belief that you are your life. And that you are at stake in doing this right, in making sure that everything is taken care of.

But the fact is that it is just not true. So it is not that you can stop doing that dance, or that you should try to do so, because that is just another aspect of the belief that I am my life, and I am doing my life wrong, I have got to do it right by stopping this stupid dance. So, it is not so much a matter of wanting to stop the dance, or wanting to stop that personally self-destructive behavior. What you want is the truth, always, in all times. You want the truth. If it is true that life is not worth living and you are despicable and unworthy, then you want to know that, because it is really you here, and the only way you can know that is to look at yourself. And when you look at yourself, then you can speak only from the truth.

When you want to reconcile and make things right, and convince your own self, along with them, that life is worth living, then you are off on the same madness, the same swamp. But you do the inquiry, look at yourself, and make that the most important thing you are doing. It will naturally follow from that that you will speak to your son and your boyfriend from the truth, and not from any scheme or strategy to maintain some idea that life is good and you are stupid.

That is all you can do. It always comes back to the same thing, it always does. So you look at yourself. You are here, you are the same. It doesn't matter whether this character is out dancing with suicidal maniacs. *(laughter)* Really, it doesn't matter, it doesn't touch you. It doesn't matter if you are able to become a light unto the world, and spread joy and peace and good feelings, that doesn't help you. You have to see that. And then it doesn't mean that the character won't continue her dance with the suicidal maniacs, or become the light upon the world, and make everybody feel good. But you will see the truth, and you will know that you are not at stake in this life, you are not at stake in this dance, and you are not at stake in these relationships. And then you can speak the straight scoop to whomever comes to you, in any circumstance whatsoever. Then you can speak straight as an arrow, and tell the truth. And then, who knows?

It is not that I am suggesting, or I am claiming that you should in any way believe that this is going to make you a more effective person, or smarter, or dumber, or better in relationships, or worse in relationships. All it is going to do is show you the truth, just that. And the way that these characters play out in this container — in reality — is beyond your control anyway. You can't do anything about it, and you know that. But I also say that once you are done with the lie, if you want to become a more effective personality, you have got a much better chance of pulling it off. Okay? *(laughter)*

Sure. Because it is only in the moment, anyway. It's only in the moment. Thank you.

You are welcome. Anybody else? It is a lot easier for me if you guys just come up and tell me what you want to hear, rather than me trying to figure out what I should say. Yes? That was a very tentative hand, but I caught you. *(laughter)*

∽

Hi. I feel like I am being redundant again.

It's okay. Nobody could be more redundant than me. *(laughter)*

Spontaneously, I am aware a little bit here and there. Not often, it hasn't happened many times. Only one time very clearly have I felt aware of awareness. But it has never happened while I am doing the inquiry. And so, when you are saying to try to get to a certain place, or that you will be familiar with what it is, that has never happened when I am trying to do the inquiry. That makes me feel like I don't know what to do. Can the response be spontaneous and not happen when I am trying to do it?

Of course, if you turn the heat on under a pot of water, it doesn't start boiling right away, right? It takes a while. You can walk away from it, and after a while it starts boiling. That is not a very good metaphor, but it is just the first one that came to mind. Yes, of course. The thing to do is to look, and the looking does all the work. Your intentional looking for what you are does all the work, and the result of that is quite often spontaneous, seemingly unconnected flashes of "Oh, that!"

The truth is that no present effort that you are undertaking to see the reality of what you are will bear fruit in that effort. I am really glad you brought this up. Remember when I talked about how I sat on my bed, and fought and struggled? The seeing comes outside of the arena of the struggle. The struggle is certainly the catalyst for it. If you stop trying to look at yourself, you will miss it when it comes.

Every second, every nanosecond, without any interruption whatsoever, you are always fully aware of awareness, which is what you are. There is never a single heartbeat, a hair's breadth of time when you are not fully aware of awareness. The only thing about it is that you don't see that that is the case, because you are looking for something else. Looking here, looking there, wanting this, wanting that, wanting the other thing, never suspecting that what you really want more than anything else, you already are seeing, having, being.

So, the effect of the work is to kind of create the atmosphere, the environment where, because of the fact that you are exerting yourself to try to see what you really are, when moments come when this that is permanently happening reveals itself, you see them for what they are. Whereas prior to engaging in the work itself, it is just stuff that happens. It is just "Oops, that's gone. What was that?" You might not even notice it, and it is gone. Now you see it, now you see it for what it is. And that is why the work is in the looking, the looking does it all.

And the intention.

The intention does it all. So, I think you are doing just fine. The exertion to try to see yourself is not going to give you instant gratification, or if it does, it is entirely coincidental. It just so happens that while you were doing it, there was one of those passing moments when this reality that is always here was seeable. I wasn't sure I should tell you that lest you think, "Oh, well, then I don't have to do the work." You do have to do the work. I swear to you, you do have to do the work.

Well, you don't really have to, right? You can go on marching to the grave blissfully, or not so blissfully, unaware. But if you want to be done, if you really want to love your life, if you want to be finished with misery, you have got to do the work. You have got to try with all your heart to look directly, face-to-face, nakedly, at the reality of what you are. Just to look at it, not to know it, not to understand it, not to name it, just to look at it. It is just the looking at it.

And when you try that, it comes. That is the point. If you continue trying, it comes. More and more, it comes. You will wake up in the morning and you will say, "Oh, look, yes, right. This is easy." And then you will be doing the inquiry, and you won't be making any progress, and you will be going off doing other things... You will be in the shower, and all of a sudden, you will say, "Ah. Yes. Right. Look." Or in the checkout line... More and more, more and more, cumulative. Is that helpful?

It is. Thank you.

Okay, you are welcome.

I am glad I asked.

I am glad you did, too.

I was wondering if I should wait...

No, no, that was a really good question. It was a really good thing to bring up...

I thought so.

I don't know why I had never thought of explaining that before, because it seems so obvious that it is something that we ought to know when we embark on this effort. I am not one of those teachers who think you've got to suffer. You really don't have to suffer. This is easy. This isn't something where you have to do a hundred and eight thousand prostrations just to get to know what the teaching is.

☙

I am experiencing quite a bit of silence. And I am watching also the tendency to want to fill the space. I have just been very curious about it today, and I was just sitting with it, and I wasn't sure if I wanted to get up and talk about it, for fear that the need to fill the space would just kind of fill it up too much.

This is excellent, because this is the whole point of making this a silent retreat. Sometimes I will tell you ahead of time what the point of things is, and sometimes I just forget. But the whole point of making this a silent retreat is not because there is some ooga-booga power in silence. There may be, but that is not why we have the silent retreat. The reason for making it silent is because in declining to speak, you are declining to fill the space with your chatter. And when that is occurring, the urge to fill it becomes quite apparent, so that you get to see how these things operate, how deep-seated is the habit of wanting to tell a story about what is happening, wanting to assert yourself, wanting to confirm your identity as whatever in the world you think you are. And that urge is very strong.

Well, plus it gets more and more subtle. I feel like I can experience the silence whether talking or not.

Of course, you can.

But what I was noticing sitting there was very subtle. I wanted to look at it with you. I was wanting to feel something, I was just feeling kind of nothing.

Perfect. Perfect.

And I don't know what all this emotion is about.

It doesn't matter. There is no need to know any of that. This stuff just happens. They are gifts. This emotional uprising is just a sensational gift, because it feels good to be kind of loosened up, it feels good. It is just a gift, a stroke of luck. This person deserves that, really. That doesn't help you, it doesn't have any effect on you whatsoever. You are the same, you have never changed, you are the source of it all, but this person deserves to get a little hit every once in a while.

A little hit?

A little hit, a little sweetness.

I was noticing how the silence, the truth of it felt enough, but there was this tendency of wanting more, wanting to feel more, and it was subtle. It's just very subtle.

That tendency is not a problem.

It wasn't appearing like a problem to me, I was just curious about it.

That's right, it is not a problem. It is exactly what you call it. It is a tendency, and it doesn't create any problems. Even in seeking to satisfy itself, no problem is created. You are untouched by it.

It is amazing to see that there are these patterns of energetic movement that repeat and recur, which in and of themselves comprise the shape of this person, taken together over time, as a whole. And to see that there is nothing that needs to be done about them. Who cares? It doesn't hurt anybody, it doesn't help anybody, it is just a pattern, a tendency.

Ramana said that for the jnani — I don't know why he used words like that. Ramana said that the only vasanas (a vasana is a tendency) that remain for the jnani are vasanas of enjoyment. And the truth of it is that all vasanas are vasanas of enjoyment. So that the point of this is not the destruction of these vasanic tendencies, but the freeing of them from the burden of the belief that your whole fate is riding on them. And then you see them, and they are just things. They are just the way in which reality takes form.

Right in this moment, the gratitude feels very big.

Yes, that is to be expected.

There is a preference for that silence, which was just more quiet and more simple, and seemingly more the truth. There is still this tendency to want to fill it with more of these emotional states.

Right, and the preference itself is a tendency.

Right.

And there is nothing wrong with any of that. When this fullness passes, as it will, silence remains. You remain — unaffected by it, not needing to get it back, not needing to make it go, just you, just reality, just simple you. And the seeing of that washes away all the grasping and holding away, all the "I want this," and "I don't want that," all the juice behind it.

I can just see how I was thinking that that fullness was what I was looking for.

That's right.

The big wows, and the big everything.

And we get that, and then we lament its passing, and then we try to find some other teacher or some other teaching that will give it back to us, and then we lament its passing, and then we look for something else... And most of us get trapped in that spiritual rat race of wanting to get that, wanting to hold that hit, and wanting to get hold of it. It is okay. But you are done with that.

It just feels like a different scene happening now.

Yes, you are done with that. All that brought you to the inquiry, brought you to yourself, and now you are done with that. And you will get huge, big experiences of fulfillment, and they will pass, and you will get experiences of scarcity, and wanting and not getting, and they will pass, too. But you will remain, the same as you are now, exactly the same, no different, unchanged.

Thank you.

You are very welcome. I am very happy to be in this adventure with you.

I have no idea what I am doing, but it seems to work.

And what do you think it might be that you are doing?

Looking at me.

There it is. That is what you are doing. And it does work. It is amazing, because it doesn't work in the way we expect it to, just as we were talking about it two or three minutes ago; it doesn't work the way we think it should work, but it works.

Just being me. That is all I have to be.

Yes, that's it, as if you could be anything else. Mostly that is what it entails, it is a divesting yourself of the idea that you need to be something else.

In my life I have been very good at hiding... I don't want to do this... I don't want to cry...

How is that working for you now? *(laughter)*

It's true, it doesn't work. Oh, I am crying... I felt like the world had teeth and I had died. I still find it hard to deal with other people's need to be vicious. And I used to be vicious, too...

Vicious? It will take time for that to go.

I can see the choice now. I don't have to do that anymore. But I still find it hard to be in the world, because I see that everyone is doing it, protecting themselves.

Yes, everyone is. We are all desperately trying to protect a lot, you are absolutely right about that. But you are not anymore.

No. But I have to remind myself, I can do this, I can stick with it.

That's okay, that doesn't hurt you to remind yourself of that. You keep doing what you are doing, keep up this inquiry. And your seeing is correct: that is what everybody is doing. Everybody is desperately trying to protect themselves, trying to protect an idea of themselves. And the reason that they all are doing that is the same reason that you always were doing it: an underlying seeing that it is all a lie.

Yeah, but as everyone, I didn't know what I was doing then.

Well, you didn't know you were doing that, but you were doing it as a result of a need to protect the lie. And the reason that it gets so vicious is because we know it is a lie and we have to hide that from ourselves, too.

I suppose now I can say, "Yes, I was lying big time to myself..."

But then, you couldn't.

No.

So, hallelujah. *(laughter)*

So being around that...

Being in the world, you mean?

Yeah.

What about it?

I just have to be myself, I suppose...

Yes, of course. You can't not be yourself. I tell you this, this is the truth. If you continue with the inquiry, and it is obvious that you are doing it right, all these things will be cleared up. This fearfulness about doing the right thing, and how you relate to people, these are all vestiges, just leftover stuff, and it will all be cleared up. It really will, I promise. And you know that. You have seen, startlingly, what has happened to you in the period of time you have been undertaking this practice. Everything will be cleared up. Are you from New Zealand?

Yes. I don't know if anyone knows this, but twelve people were arrested as terrorists just recently in New Zealand... I live with the mother of one of the people that were arrested. And they are just activists, that is all they are. But they are now being called terrorists. That seems to be a word that everyone wants to use. And I would like to reach out to her. I want to help to stop that pain, because she is in pain, her daughter is in pain.

You can't do anything about that. But you can tell the truth. The only thing you can ever do is tell the truth. And it may be that telling the truth means saying nothing. If you can't do anything, you just can't do anything, except love them. I mean, really, just be helpful. Don't be hurtful, be helpful. Don't serve the continuation of the lie, don't do that. Like we were talking about before, that is just serving the continuation of the lie, dancing, getting engaged with that, so you don't do that. You tell the truth. And it may mean saying almost nothing, and just caring about people, and helping them in material ways, if you can. But don't lie.

I started a conversation with her, and it just ended up being like a tennis match, and I haven't done it again. I left her a bottle of wine when I left.

That is a genuine gesture of care. Care for one another, if you can. You know, all this stuff about how we don't have anything to say about what we do, well, there is a lot of truth to that, but if you *do* have anything to say about what you do, care for each other. Help each other. And don't ever lie about reality.

It's actually really good to hear that sometimes to say nothing is telling the truth.

That's right, it is. If you have nothing to say, then saying nothing is telling the truth. And what we most often try to do is fill it up. We look and see, "Okay, what should I be saying? How should I be helping her?" Anything. You know what I mean.

Yeah, I see. Thank you.

I am very happy to see you here.

It's great to be here. You know, when I first got here, I think I was suffering from jet lag, and other things, and I thought, "What am I doing here?"

Too late, I had you then.

Even after I booked the tickets over here, I thought, "Oh, what have I done?" But it is fantastic to be here, and thank you.

You are very welcome, it's fantastic to have you here.

It is wonderful to hear everyone too, as well as on podcasts. You know they are all talking, and it's my voice…

Yes, that's right, it is very useful. These meetings are very useful. Sometimes it is not clear to me exactly why. In fact, it is never really clear to me exactly why, although I could make up an explanation for it, but these gatherings are very useful. It is very helpful to see each other face-to-face.

And I also appreciate that you don't talk about the crap that I create, you know? My life and what I think. I really appreciate the fact that I really get it that it's just beside the point.

Yes, that's it, exactly, beside the point. We drive ourselves crazy as we peter away our entire lives trying to do something about the crap.

And that's exactly what I have done.

That is what we all have done. But no more.

No. It is just amazing.

Let the crap take care of itself.

It just goes on. It is quite happy.

It is good to see you.

Thank you.

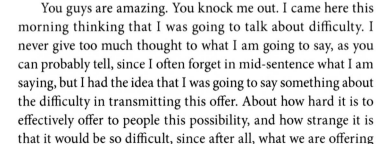

You guys are amazing. You knock me out. I came here this morning thinking that I was going to talk about difficulty. I never give too much thought to what I am going to say, as you can probably tell, since I often forget in mid-sentence what I am saying, but I had the idea that I was going to say something about the difficulty in transmitting this offer. About how hard it is to effectively offer to people this possibility, and how strange it is that it would be so difficult, since after all, what we are offering is the secret of eternal happiness. You would think there would be a market for that, especially when it is free. *(laughter)*

And I imagine that I probably would have said something about the prevalence and the predominance of the culture of instant gratification. We read a book because it feels good to read a book, and we go to a movie because it feels good to go to a movie, and we eat good food for the same reason. We hang out with our friends because it feels good. We get high because it feels

135

good. And we have always had this tendency toward preferring instant gratification rather than deferred gratification. We are all just children with infantile ideas of how we should be served by the world. And that tendency toward instant gratification has become writ large in our lifetime, in this time when we can instantly watch a movie, instantly get what we want. You go to Amazon.com, and in one click, bing bang boom, you get whatever it was you wanted to buy. You don't even have to get out of bed, really. *(laughter)* And I guess I would have lamented all that as burdens on us, when confronted with the so simple, so accessible, so uncomplicated possibility of being finished with wanting and not getting, yearning and not being satisfied, thirsting and not finding water.

I have said before that Ramana always said that this teaching, this practice is for the very few, the very sharpest few. But look at me. I am definitely not the sharpest knife in the drawer. Look at my history, look at the way I have lived my life. So if it is accessible to me, then Ramana must be wrong, it must be accessible to everybody. Maybe he was right, but he just had the wrong criterion for what it takes. Maybe it's not sharpness, maybe desperation is what it takes. And maybe we are just not desperate enough to try something so simple, and so lacking the instant hit of gratification that self-inquiry is. It doesn't give you this "Ah!" It gives you yourself, just as you are, simple, unadorned, reality itself. So maybe one who is not really desperate, who is not really caught up in the depths, the swamp, the cesspool of spiritual psycho-suffering melodrama cannot get this. You have to really be stupid to get it. It is not that you have to really be smart, you have to really be stupid to get it, really stupid. *(laughter)*

Anyway, these are the kind of things that were running in this mind this morning. This mind is a source of endless amusement to me, and the things it says and talks about to itself. And then I come here, and I ask, Does anybody here have anything to say? And I hear these heartbreaking, stunningly beautiful and authentic reports and questions and discussions and conversations, and I say to myself, What could I be thinking? This is for all, this is for everybody — the smart, the stupid, the brave, the coward. It is for everybody, every human being.

Every human being absolutely has the capacity in this moment to know the reality of what they are, and in that knowing, to be free of misery and suffering in this life. Every human being has the capacity to see this and have their life seemingly redeemed, and have their life reveal itself to be everything they have ever wanted. Everything, just as it is. Every human being can do this. None of us are so smart or so dumb that we can't see what we are. None of us are so self-satisfied or so sunk in a swamp of psycho-spiritual suffering that we can't see this reality, just for a moment.

Just for a moment, what are you? Just for a moment, are you not absolutely certain that you *are*? Is this not true for you? Just now ask yourself, have you ever changed? Are you not the same now as you were when you were three years old? Have you really, ever been touched, affected or scarred by any of the occurrences in your life? Have you ever been enhanced by anything you have received, or diminished by anything you have lost? Really, look and see. And in the looking there, in the looking to find what is true, what is real, in the looking to see what you are, everything else is taken care of. Everything.

And the magnificent thing about the inquiry is that once it is started, it continues on its own, it really does. Once it is started, it continues on its own. That is part of what you are reporting, the fact that it continues on its own. Once it is started, once the clarity appears as to what it is you are looking for, once you get the first, conscious seeing, knowing, "Oh, that's it, that is what I'm looking for..." It may be hours after practicing the inquiry, "Oh, that's it, that's it." Once you get that, it will drag you down into the truth. Once you get that, there is no turning back.

So here I am, all optimistic again. *(laughter)* I can't tell you how wonderful it is to be with you in this retreat. Really, there is no way in the world that I can convey to you how wonderful it is to be here with you, to see you, to speak with you, to hear what you have to say. The truth is, I swear to god, we are all in this together. We are going to sink or swim together.

Okay. Have a good lunch. Enjoy yourself. Look at yourself. Never forget yourself. If you forget yourself, remember yourself. And I guess I will be back at five, god willing, and if the creek don't rise. Thank you so much for your time.

Okay, one more.

☯

I will stop anything for you.

That's very sweet. I just wanted to disagree with you.

About?

You said something about instant gratification and delayed gratification and for me, it is definitely instant gratification. And it is just sitting in the room, it is just little mini-hits of bliss. But nothing changed.

Yes, that's right. That's it.

I guess that is the thing: it's becoming aware of...

But you have been doing this for a while...

What has happened is when I started doing this, life became so much better that I started enjoying all those other pursuits. So it became very easy to get trapped in all those other pursuits, if I use that to look at it. And the value of coming back and saying, "All right, this is where the pleasure really originates from..."

Yes, that's right.

Again, it's an instant gratification, that's all.

Well, I am glad you are getting instant gratification. I am glad you are here. It is really good to stay, to come back.

I am sometimes a little embarrassed that I feel the need to come back. I think, "You know, I should be done with this."

Says who? I am not done with it.

No.

Okay?

It's so beautiful.

Okay. I love you all, really, with all my heart. Thank you for this meeting. Thank you for this time together. I will see you at five o'clock. Enjoy yourself.

Look At Yourself

Meeting 7

November 5, 2007 - Afternoon

Sometimes I really hate to start speaking, because it is so sweet here without speaking. But then, my tendencies take over and I am off and running. Does anybody want to come and talk to me?

I have a question about our last session. Everybody that spoke, it was as if they were speaking for me and I could feel what they were saying, it was as if they were my mouthpiece. Is that what you mean with one mind?

Well, it might be. But there are other things to take into consideration, too. We are all in the same boat. We think that our take on things, and the particular shape of our confusion and our realization, when it comes, that they are all very personal, and individual to 'me'. There is a strong belief in play that I am unique as this personality. And in some ways that is true, the personalities are unique, in the same way that every dandelion is absolutely unique, although they all look the same. So, it comes as no surprise, and it doesn't take the intervention of a spiritual explanation for it, to see that once we are in an environment and in a setting where it is possible to speak about these things that we speak about here, that the people who are speaking would be speaking exactly as if they were you, because we really are all in the same boat. For all of us, there really is only this one issue, there is no other issue. And the beginning of the breaking of that issue, for all of us, produces the same kind of effects, and consequences, and results, and reports.

The other part of it is that we really don't have a wide range of ways in which to express ourselves. Although the experiences people report might be extremely unique, but very subtly so, when we try to talk about it, we only have these clunky words to use to talk about it, so that it is to be expected that we would have the same thing to say as you have. But it is also true that there is only one mind, that's true, too. And all these things that I have pointed out are characteristics of the fact that there is only one mind. So, I don't know how to answer that question.

Well, then, could you also say there is only one heart?

Sure, it's the same thing.

Okay, because this laughing and crying stuff, I wondered about that... What is that?

It's just a release; it is just something being released. We tell a story about what it is, but it is just something that we release, some breaking of a previous calcification, that's all.

When you were talking about compassion, is that like feeling pain with another person as they are expressing themselves?

Yes, their pain is your pain. And it is not something that you seek out. It seems like it is a bug, not a feature. I mean, if anybody had the choice, if I had the choice, and I could have somebody come down from heaven and strike me on the forehead and have me completely clear and absolutely filled with grace and silence and clarity and no confusion, without regard to whether you were all twisted up, I probably would take it, right? I mean, life is short. *(laughter)*

But it is just not the case. The truth is that we are all in this together, and the truth is that your pain is my pain. There is no separation, there is no boundary, and that is part of the practical reason for the development of this belief in me as being endangered by my life, and separate from you and isolated from you, on my own. Part of the reason that this belief develops until it is so strong and so difficult to even see, much less dislodge, is because of its utility, because it keeps me in the idea that your pain is your pain, and that it doesn't touch me, it doesn't affect me, even though that is not true. Even when I am sound asleep in this belief, it still produces that kind of illusion that I have defense against you and your craziness.

And I could just as easily talk about this in sweeter and more loving terms, but I don't do so because I think it is really important to see that compassion, like everything else, isn't what we think it is, that it is not some characteristic of sweetness and light and love. It is a practical aspect of life as a human being. Compassion is not something we choose; it is something we spend most of our life trying desperately to get rid of. So, that's what I say. And as long as we are talking about compassion, we might as well take on love, also.

Love isn't what we think it is. We are very fond of the spiritual utterances about love, and eternal love, and infinite love, and all is love, and all that is true. And we think we know what love is, but we don't have a clue what love is. We think love is the spiritual counterpart, or the spiritual equivalent of the emotional madness that strikes us as human beings, either as parents of children, or children of parents, or lovers of lovers. There is this madness that strikes us when the presence of someone in our life becomes critically important to us. There is an emotional component to it that is very big. The emotional component kind of relaxes over time, but it is very big. That is not the love of reality, it's not. It is a characteristic of human attachment and the human desire to have what I want and get rid of what I don't want. And it is quite a miracle that despite its essential, selfish root, it leads to such magnificent, beautiful relationships in the world. It is a miracle that that should happen.

But even the beautiful and miraculous love relationships that actually flourish and take root in the world against all odds, relationships that are sweet, and pure and true, even that is not the love of reality. That is like candy. The love that is spoken of by the sages, the love that is spoken of by the great ones throughout time is the love that absolutely doesn't care. That is what makes it universal and unconditional. It absolutely has no care component to it at all; it has no capacity to make a judgment, to judge whether you are good or bad, whether you are well or not well, whether you are worthy of love or unworthy of love, whether you are saint or sinner, murderer or healer. It doesn't have any of those characteristics; its light shines, with absolute impartiality, on all. It gives life to all, without condition. So, that's love without condition. Love without condition is love that doesn't care, it welcomes everything, it doesn't want to fix anything, it doesn't want to keep anything from being fixed, and that is you.

That makes me very happy. My husband said to me the other day, "You don't care about anything, do you?" (laughter)

Yes, and that is a feature, not a bug.

So, there you go!

There you go. *(laughter)*

And it seems that the laughing is just like such relief!

It is relief... It is a great relief.

It isn't what I thought it was...

That's right.

It is like…

Whew! I had that one wrong. Thank god!

Yeah. I finally got the joke. Wow! That is a good joke!

Yes, that's it. It's a good joke. It's a good joke once you get the punch line. It is not so good when you think you are trapped in it.

Yes. Thank you.

You are very welcome. You are beautiful, you really are.

Thanks, John.

෨

It has been and continues to be a real gift to dive into self-inquiry in an intense setting like this, and I am realizing that before, I only flirted with it. And now…

That's the value of a retreat, to really see what it is about.

So it feels like it has taken hold, and I feel like I will be engaged with it in a new way. I already am… And I can feel some sense of certainty that that will continue.

That's good. It will.

And now that I feel us coming to the end of the retreat, I have some nuts and bolts questions about self-inquiry. As I find myself doing it, I notice that there are lots of different ways that I enter into it. And it kind of feels like the most naked way is probably the best, but I can't always do that. Sometimes I'll say, "Well, I'm not there right now. Who's feeling that difficulty?" Those kinds of "who is" questions...

Or even, in the midst of difficulty, is there something here that is not touched by this difficulty, that is not disturbed by this disturbance?

Are those mental exercises, those mental introductions into the practice positive, are those okay? Or is it good to just strip those away?

Anything is okay. Anything that is done with the intent to come face-to-face with the reality of what you are is fine. The two most amazing things about this practice are that nobody can tell you how to do it, and that you can't do it wrong. Intent is everything in this. And if the intent is there to see face-to-face the naked reality of what you are, without any understanding, then whatever you do will bring you to that. That is the truth. You have to see that the whole impetus and the activity itself of the inquiry reside within this belief that I am my life. It is a part of this limitation, it is not outside of that. It occurs within this personality, within this apparatus. Somehow, within this apparatus, has appeared this desire to be free of the belief that I am this apparatus. But all of that happens within the story of me, including the inquiry. Where else would it come from? In truth, you know what you are. You have never not known what you are. It certainly can't be coming from you, you are not confused about that. It comes from this strange creature.

When you said this morning that there is never a nanosecond when we are not aware of that, that helped a lot, because one of the places I was getting stuck was the sense that I am not doing this right, I am not doing self-inquiry right now, and you were saying that self-inquiry, in a sense, is always happening.

Yes, that's right. The main object of your awareness is always itself. Always.

How could I not be seeing anything if it is lighting all this? So it is always at work, always there, always by my side.

That's right. I used to think that if I repeat myself, I am boring people, but I have learned that I really do need to repeat myself, that sometimes people hear things the first time I say it, and sometimes they hear it the hundred-and-fifteenth time I say it.

The last piece that I wanted to ask you about is having that inquiry deepen and expand and broaden.

Where would it go?

Well, I trust that that will happen naturally.

Where would it go? How would it broaden? Where would it broaden to? What would it broaden into? I mean, it's you...

It would push out all these thoughts and the desire to understand...

What is the problem with the thoughts? You are the source of the thoughts.

But as you have practiced this, hasn't that expanded for you to the point where you are able to talk about it as you are? I mean, you started self-inquiry many, many years ago, and it probably had a faltering kind of quality...

It had a crazy kind of quality. Weren't you here when I was talking about that? It was insane, it was absolutely insane. You really can't do it wrong. And the idea that there is some depth to you that needs to be plumbed is absurd. You are just you. Depth is some idea that you may project upon reality, but reality has no depth, nor height, nor breadth. Reality is a singularity, it encompasses all. It certainly is true that over time, this creature, in this life, gets a little bit better about talking about it, but that is just like learning to play a guitar. It is no big thing.

So be here with what is and don't worry so much about the future.

That's right. Where is the future? The only thing that is asked of you is that you, whenever you can, look at yourself, try with all your heart to look at yourself, that's all. The rest of it, you don't have anything to say about.

I realize that I am in a way kind of asking you for tips, which is all about the how-to, and this isn't really about how-to, it's about letting go.

The only how-to I can provide you with is the encouragement to look at yourself. Turn your attention backwards, find the subject, look for the seer, look for what is permanent. The more that I need to say in order to provide you with some direction, the further away we get from the actual object of the practice. The more that I say, the further we get from it, which is not to say that there is no point in me saying more, and I do say more, god knows I say a lot. But just to see that even though it may be necessary, that kind of discourse about how it happens and what you do, the more we talk about it, the further away we get from it. You are here, and that's the whole deal. The rest of it is commentary.

Well, I'd like to officially retract my previous statement that I don't agree with you about how hard it is. It does feel pretty natural. It feels very natural as I dive into it.

It has been a pleasure to be with you on this retreat.

It has been a pleasure to be with all of you on this retreat. Wait a minute, there was somebody else…

I went on a six-mile hike today for the first time and I also went to church, because I had a responsibility to play the harmonium, and I just wanted to share with you that my life has literally completely changed, and I know you can see that. It's just amazing. I like what you just said, how you keep it so simple, because it is. And it's so truthful that if you continue to talk, that is just more of the story. Because when my friend used to talk to me, I would get so mad at her, because I would be having a stomach ache, having anxiety, depression, "Oh, I just want to die, I don't like this! My life is terrible!" You know, the whole drama. I loved that drama. And now, it's like, "Man, I've got to find other things to do that are fun, because so much of this illusion and drama, and 'I am victim' and 'Oh, this person did this to me', and all these things, and even the past that we have had with our gurus and our teachers. God bless all of it, because it has led us to this point right here." So, my only question is, what would be the best way that I can share this with others, in the process of doing it myself? Maybe that is the best way, just to continue doing it myself...

That's the best way, that's right.

And it seems like it speaks without words...

That's right, and that is the best way. I will tell you the truth. When you are downtown at the market, people are touched by you. You don't know it, they might not even know it, but they are, and the best thing you can do for the foreseeable future is to keep up the inquiry. And whatever you are called upon to do will be quite obvious. You don't need to think about these things.

You're right. I have often wondered, I have been kind of hyper, and talkative, and dramatic. And it's just so amazing that I have just found a peace, it's just incredible! The six-mile hike today, I was able to share it with my friend, and we did our prayers, and she was saying, "And all the ascended masters..." and "May we feel the presence of god," and all these things that I used to love and actually I still do, because it's all fun. But I said, "Well, all that stuff is nice, but, what about..." I pointed right back at me, and it was so exciting, because I didn't even want the sparks in the sky and the kundalini rushing up the spine. I didn't even want that. I just wanted to sit with myself.

You are so beautiful!

So, thank you, John, both of you guys. I just want to cry. You guys are amazing. I am going to suggest this so highly to everyone that is sitting rocking out to the kirtans... You know what? Can you sit with yourself? Go to John! (laughter) Thank you, John.

You are so welcome. *(laughter)* Nothing at all that I can say about that...

രാ

Hello.

So I have been doing the inquiry. I guess I started in May. I saw you in Chicago, and I think right after I saw you, I had the kind of experience you are talking about where I see what you are pointing at, and things take care of themselves, they start to take care of themselves after that. And I think in a lot of ways, I just want to say that you have done your job, and it has kind of just taken me completely and I see that this is what I want, this is what I'm doing...

That's it. That's it.

So the other part is, and maybe you will be a little sad about it, it has been pretty melodramatic. But it doesn't seem like really a problem...

It is not a problem. Nobody was more melodramatic with this than I was. I don't think there is anybody that could possibly be more stirred up in a spiritual melodrama than I was. It doesn't matter, it really doesn't.

It doesn't. It's kind of silly, I am a little embarrassed about it, but I have just been spending quite some time the past couple days trying to figure out what I could report to you, and it's like, "Man, I do not need to or want to talk about any of the melodrama." It just doesn't feel real at all. It's real enough to have the thought about it, and that is it. I have all these drafts of emails to you, but I haven't been able to report anything to you, because this melodrama stuff is just nothing.

That's great good news, really. And it really doesn't matter, it just comes and goes. And that is one of the most important things that differentiate this teaching from pretty much all other teachings. Although others might say, "The melodrama isn't it," they nevertheless will make a big deal of it, like, "You've got to stop it." "You've got to get rid of the melodrama." But in this inquiry, there is no such thing as that. Melodrama is welcome, no melodrama is welcome. You are here.

I guess I thought maybe it would be worthwhile to say a couple of things about the things you have said that have really helped me start doing it.

That would be worthwhile.

All this stuff about intent was scary at first. How do I know if I have the right motivation to do it? Is this really what I want? Do I really want to see what I am? It's kind of scary, almost... And then, am I desperate enough for it? Am I really at the end of my rope? And then you said things like, you could do it to get rich, or lose weight or whatever, to get high. (laughter) And it does feel good, so I just started doing it. That question about whether I am ready for it, or right for it, you took that away from me. I can't fight with you, you just keep taking these things away from me, you know? (laughter)

And the thing is, as you can see, when I say 'intent', because we so know what spiritual intent should be, we think that means something in particular, but it doesn't. It is the intent that counts, it is not what story you are telling about the intent, like "I am going to do it so I can get high," or "I am going to do it so I can get rich," or "I am going to do it so I can get laid." Or "I am going to do it so I can be the Buddha." The story you are telling about the intent is beside the point.

Right. That's the other thing you said: "This is what you want. You may not realize it, and if you don't, you should pretend that it is what you want." So you just took everything I had to fight it away from me. I just had to do it, even with melodrama, I just had to keep coming back to it. And I have. Maybe I'll go into the melodrama at some point, I just don't think I could do that and feel genuine about it. I thought I had some questions, but you took my questions away when you started talking today. I haven't heard you say this before, but you started talking about the importance of your native intelligence, your native common sense about it, so I had some questions about confirmation and different kinds of things that are going on, and I just don't think I have those anymore.

That's good news.

Thanks.

You are very welcome. I am really happy to see you.

I am glad to be here. I am glad to be, you know? I am glad you tricked me into this adventure. (laughter) It has been kind of crazy, like I said, but...

Here you are.

Yes.

Here you remain.

Thanks.

Oh, this is great news, thank you.

∞

As long as we are talking about melodramas... I got a little freaked out. Not totally freaked out, but a little bit...

When?

Just in the course of the retreat, I think after yesterday's conversation, when you were referring to yourself, saying "John is here, and John is there," and sort of seeing again that everybody is me, and that all of that stuff and crap that I have been working so diligently to rid myself of... And then the realization that there is a lot of it out there and one of my strategies is just to run away and hide from it all. So I just was sort of in that, the bells and the whistles going "Beep, beep! Danger! Danger!" Not only about my stuff, but just dealing with other people's stuff. So the question was, "Who is at stake?"

Right. Good question.

Because there is a lot of stuff going on in the sensational realm, still some anxiety, and fear, and how am I going to deal with another person's stuff? And who is at stake?

You don't even have to deal with your stuff, much less anybody else's stuff. All you have to do is look at yourself, and let the light in. That is all you have to do, everything else will be taken care of. All this stuff-dealing is taken care of, you really don't have to do anything about it, I promise.

I'm getting to see that. But some of it seems so immediate, and when there is a reaction in the body, the inclination is to think I have to do something about it.

And that's okay, really, even that can't hurt you, nor can it keep you from the inquiry. It is not like that is wrong, and that prevents you from doing anything. The most bone-headed impulses that you follow can't hurt you, and they can't help you, and they can't prevent you from seeing that, in the midst of all of this, you are here. Unmoved, unchanged, the same. And when you see that, then you can see that these very impulses and the freaking out, and all the wrongheaded stuff actually is your ally, because against the backdrop of that craziness, you can see the unchanging, unmoving, permanent reality of you starkly, because it is so different from this jingle jangle wildness.

Yeah, that was almost like a bell to remind me that I had moved away. That's not even the right way to put it…

Just to remind you. You are doing fine.

It seems like there was just a lot of contraction in the body. It was really hard to hang with it.

But you don't have to. Even if you fight it, it is okay. Those of us who have been conditioned in the spiritual realm have this idea that some of these things have to be dealt with, or else I won't attain what I am trying to attain. But that is just a lie, it is just not true. You can fight it, you can do the stupidest thing you can think about, whatever that might be, the most unspiritual, the most contracted, the most not true, and it doesn't touch you. It can't hurt you, really. When it goes, you remain. When all the madness goes, you are still here, and you can verify that. And, after a time, either the madness calms down, or you just don't care about it. You just have to see that this madness is all thought. It is not anything being acted out in the community, it is all thought.

What I was doing also, because I have had a lot of people around this weekend, was that I was sort of watching the thought that I am not supposed to go into judgment, or that I am supposed to do this, or supposed to do that... But if I have those nasty, judgment thoughts...

Who cares?

Yes. But there is a whole school of thought that you are not supposed to judge.

Oh, yes, there is. And it is a huge burdeñ. This spiritual burden is huge that we have taken upon ourselves. I am not to be judgmental; the only thing I am allowed to be judgmental about is my judgmentalness. And that is okay, but no other judgment. *(laughter)* None of that touches you, none of it. There is no need for you to continue being judgmental, there is no need for you to leave off being judgmental. There is no need for you to continue thinking you are wrong because you are judgmental, and there is no reason for you to stop thinking you are wrong because you are judgmental. All of that is beside the point, all of it.

I see that, and there is a place where I continually get caught, and that's the thought that I am doing something wrong, that I am not doing it right. That's still an investment in the life...

You will get over that. That will go away. It will. You just keep up the inquiry, and all of that will be taken care of. None of it touches you, even being caught up doesn't touch you. You remain, as always.

A lot of the activity that I do, it's just wanting to be a better human being, but even that impulse to want to be a good person and treat other people well, even that doesn't really matter...

It doesn't matter. I think I said this earlier today. In the absence of this belief that you are at stake in this life, your chances of being a good human being and good to people are a lot better than they ever were in the past. It is that underlying sense that I am at stake here, which itself can give rise to the effort to be a good human being and be good to people, that causes all the trouble. But you don't have to do anything about any of that. All you have to do is rid yourself of this lie. And the only thing you can do to rid yourself of this lie is try with all your heart to look at the reality of what you are, repeatedly, again and again. And you can see for yourself the effect it has had on you already. I can see it. We have known each other for a long time, and I see the difference.

There is another level to it that came up also. I do have a big fear that humankind, that we are not going to make it. I care, but even having a stake in that, I can't even do that.

No, you can't.

I get very upset.

The best thing you can do for humanity is to rid yourself of the lie. Because it is really true that we are all in the same boat, and that cuts in both ways: the presence in all of us of the craziness of all of us, and also the presence in all of us of a modicum of sanity when it dawns in any of us. The only thing you can do is rid yourself of this lie. It is the only hope for this whole experiment of human beings, of human consciousness.

There is a place in me, when we are talking about compassion, I guess it's the thought that if I don't care, or I am not invested, then I am going to become coldhearted, or I won't be able to really be compassionate. That's just a mind thing.

That is just because of the misunderstanding about compassion. And if you are to be coldhearted, nothing you can do will change that. If it is the nature of this personality to be coldhearted, there is nothing you can do to make that change. If it is in the nature of this person to be warmhearted, there is no power on Earth that you can bring to bear that will change that. And the actual fact is that you are this love without condition. It is the light of awareness in which coldhearted and warmhearted alike live and move and have their being. That is the actual fact of it, and what happens with this character, and how she turns out in this story is out of your hands anyway.

That's a big relief. Less work to do.

It can be.

You spoke a few times about just telling the truth when you are with other people, and I am not really sure how to do that.

If you are not sure how to do it, then just don't speak. When you are in a situation that seems to call for you to say something about it, or to comment on it, if you don't know what the truth of it is, just don't say anything. That is telling the truth. Our inclination is to jump in and bring to bear all that we have learned, and that we think is good, and what should be done, and how we think things should look, but that is not telling the truth, that is just bringing to bear this whole shopping bag of ideas and thoughts and stories. So the best thing to do, if you don't know anything else to do, is to just shut up.

You don't want to reinforce any of that other stuff.

That's right. And if you do, if that happens, don't worry about it. Your number one goal is to look at yourself, as often as you can. In your relations with other people, your only goal is to tell the truth. And you will not do that, you will fail to do that many, many times. It doesn't matter. It's the intent. And the less there is in you of the remnants of this belief that you are at stake in this life, the more difficult it will be even to think about telling some story to somebody about what they should do, or what they shouldn't do, or what is happening or what isn't happening.

There is just so much of everyday investment in the life and the details, and it's just kind of an ongoing remembering what I am not.

All you really have to do is continue the practice. That will take care of it. That takes care of everything. There is no need for you to exercise yourself by trying to remember what you should be doing, or what you shouldn't be doing. There is no need for you to be part of that at all, because the truth is that the life lives itself. Your relationships with other people actually live themselves, and the only goal you can have is to see the truth and to tell the truth. That's it. And you don't have to hold things together. Things don't hold together, for one thing, and to the extent that they do, they do so despite your best intent to help them along. Okay?

Thank you.

You are welcome. I am so happy to be in this with you.

Thank you for having this retreat.

Hi, John.

I'm happy to see you.

Me, too. Now I don't know what to say.

I get that all the time... *(laughter)*

There is something that is kind of funny. I have done several retreats with you, and several times during several successive retreats, I come to the retreat, and then I start listening to you, and then I realize, John is talking about self-inquiry, and I am doing it all wrong. I mean, I screwed up, big time. When I came, I knew what it was about, but I listen to you, and then I see it is totally wrong. So I go about straightening it, making it all right. And then, one or two days later, everything is fine, there is no problem anymore. Now the same thing happened this time, and then, at some point, I was seeing this character screwing up, and then, later on, I was seeing him doing it right. And at some point, I realized, Well, actually, what does it matter? I am just seeing what is happening to this character...

That's right. He is doing it right, he is doing it wrong, you remain as always. Yes, that's true. That's the inquiry.

And I wanted to speak about some things I heard you say that I really like. One of them is when you talk about being at stake in the life, or not being at stake in the life. To me, when I was seeing this character screwing up and this character getting it right, at some point, I thought, Well, so what?

That's right, so what? That's right. If you are not at stake in it, what is it to you?

And also, there is another thing that you said that I thought was really good about the goal of the inquiry. You said the goal of the inquiry is just to look, the goal of the inquiry is just the inquiry. Somehow it removes all tension, all effort. I mean, it just seems to me that the inquiry is the inquiry. I can't get it wrong.

That's right, that's right. It is very good that you heard that so clearly, because it is something I don't really know how to say. But it is true, the only goal of the inquiry is to look, and everything else is taken care of. That is the whole point, to look. Not to see, even; just to look.

Thank you.

You are very welcome. Yes, indeed. Thank you. I am glad to be with you.

∽

You might have kind of answered my question just this last moment, but I wanted to come up and make sure.

Okay.

I felt a little nervous to come up because I guess what I wanted to bring up was some doubts about the process, rather than the flow.

That's good. I am happy to hear doubts.

I was just curious whether that was okay. So, in the process of my inquiry, or looking to see what I am, when I look, to the best of my ability, to see what I truly am, quite honestly, it seems to me that there is just nobody there. And so, I've also heard a lot about a sense that if you can truly see who you are, then you feel this sense of love and permanence and all these things...

I never said that. If I said that, I should be slapped. I never intended to say that. *(laughter)* How interesting it is that you should say, "When I look to discover what I am, there is nobody there." What about this 'I' that is looking and finding nobody there? What is that? No matter what is going on, you are here. The one thing that is common to everything is you, even to the discovery of some absence. It is you who discovers the absence.

Are you sure?

Who else, for god's sake? It's not me. *(laughter)*

But when I look, when I really try to look to see who is noticing the resistance, I don't have a sense of that.

Of what?

I don't know.

You are here, aren't you?

I am not sure.

You are not sure you are here?

I know I am supposed to be sure that I am here...

No, no, no, I don't care. You don't have to be sure you are here. But I am just really kind of surprised that you could say that.

I could say I feel my body, I feel sensations, I see things...

Yes, but stay with me here... "I" feel my body, "I" feel sensations, "I" see things...

I know the language says that, but when I look...

That is more than language. Look and see. From whence does that report come? Where is it coming from? Is it coming from the body? Is it coming from the sensations in the body that you are using as evidence that you exist? Is it coming from outside in the room somewhere?

I can't find where it is coming from.

Look. That is the point. Look.

The last thing you said to the person before me was that it is just the looking...

That's right.

Not what you see.

That's right.

So that's clear, that's fine. But there also was a feeling of being a little left out today, that there were a lot of reports of "Wow!" And I couldn't say anything like that.

But you don't have to.

And I felt a little resistance coming up because when I look, I see nobody. And I also remember past insights like, "Wow! Nobody is great! Then there is no problem!" But then, not feeling that right now, it's a little dull, my looking feels a little dull. Then I thought, "Well, to continue with it, it sort of requires faith," and then I have a whole slew of... Like my sister might say, "If you just hand your life over to Jesus, everything will be taken care of." (laughter) And so, I have always resisted that. I am not really resisting this because, why not look?

That's my question. Why not look?

Yes, why not?

You don't have to take anything on faith, you just have to look. You don't even have to look, because the actual fact of the matter is that, whether you remain in the belief that you are this life, or rid yourself of the belief that you are this life, you are the same. You are absolutely untouched. There is nothing whatsoever that has scratched you, hurt you, diminished you, or enhanced you in this entire life. So, even if you just remain convinced that you are the body, and the life, and the fighting with the things that go on...

I am still not convinced of that, either. I am just curious...

You can't hurt yourself. You are here, you are absolutely here. You have never moved. Look and see. Look at this. You are here.

You are the same as you have always been. You are this presence, this sense of being present. That is here, that doesn't change. It doesn't go away, it doesn't get bigger, it doesn't get smaller. It is you. It is ordinary. It is you. And I promise you, if you will just look, everything else will be cleared up, it will.

You say that, and it is convincing, and I have no reason not to do it, so I don't have any argument with it.

Exactly. It is not like I am asking you to give up your first-born child. I am asking you to look at yourself.

I don't have a problem with that, but I just wanted to raise it. And I had one other slight question, but it is okay if you don't want me to ask any more questions.

I want all your questions.

It has to do with choice. Is there really a choice in this?

Does it matter?

That is a good question.

That is another one of those spiritual issues. It doesn't matter. If it feels like choice, choose right, that's all. It doesn't matter. And if there is no choice, then here you are, conducting the inquiry in the midst of all your resistance, and all of your confusion, and all of your wondering...

You are right, it doesn't matter.

Who cares?

I don't care.

You see?

Yes. The looking, just looking... What about when you hear crickets chirping, or just listening, and seeing...

I used to use the word "listening" as my verb of choice, because listening has a passivity to it that is in the real nature of the inquiry. But the inquiry can also seem quite active and quite aggressive, even. And, in my case, it took the form of a very aggressive and active search for something to get rid of the pain. But in the final analysis, the actual receiving of the reality is very passive, much like listening.

So listening could be another word for looking.

Yes, it's just another word.

Because I have done a lot of wrestling with it... I told you I studied a lot of Krishnamurti — not that he recommended wrestling — but I did a lot of wrestling with things, and listening feels easier to rest into, in a way. You are sort of alert, but...

That is one of the ways to do the inquiry, just to fall back into what is always here. The means and methods are beside the point. The only thing that counts is the intent. And the intent is not like a holy intent, or a spiritual intent, it is just the intent to see yourself, to come face-to-face with the naked reality of yourself. And whatever you do to serve that intent will take you home. Really, whatever you do. Some methods may take longer, some methods may take less time, but the method that ends up carrying you to where you want to be, there is nothing you can do about it. You can't choose a faster method, or a better method. It is the intent.

Yes, that's good, that's clear to me.

The intent to get the naked apperception of reality.

The intent almost seems like the same as the looking, it has the same feeling to it.

Yes, that's right.

Without worrying about the object of it, really.

That's right. That's right.

Thank you.

Okay. And keep in touch with me. Let me know, okay?

Yes, thank you.

If anybody thinks I don't want to talk about doubts, please wipe that out of your mind. I really love to hear the reports of the effectiveness, and the actual power of this practice in people's lives, but it is almost more useful to me to hear the doubts and the resistance, because it is kind of my job to help people see, to help people come face-to-face with this reality, and the more I get to speak with you about the things that you think are off, or wrong, or how you can't do it, the better I get at my job. The better I get at serving you. That is what I really am, I am your servant.

I am *your* servant. At your service, ma'am. *(laughter)*

Thank you. I am here just because there was something that came up yesterday that I was struggling with through the night. I didn't really understand it, but I think I have got it now, and I need to just run it by you to see that I am clear on it. You were talking about telling the truth yesterday, and I thought, "Well, I tell the truth, I am an honest person." And then, you were talking about being engaged or withdrawing, and I thought, "Whoa, that may be where I don't tell the truth, because of fear of the outcome, and being attached to this." So, in other words, telling the truth at all times is detaching from the outcome of what is going to affect this person.

Yes, that's right. But I don't really advise that you tell the truth at all times. There are a lot of circumstances where it is a lot better to tell a lie. But when you are in a relationship with people, in which the issues are real (and not unreal, like so many of the things we lie about), then the only thing you can do is tell the truth, as best you can. And the more you are resolved to tell the truth, the more you see that there is not much to say to tell the truth. And sometimes, the more you resolve to tell the truth, the more you see how accustomed you are to lying, to telling stories, to weaving a point of view, the idea of what it should be and what it shouldn't be. And sometimes that just makes you be quiet; it just makes you shut up.

And you won't succeed, you see? It's kind of like the inquiry. The point of the inquiry is not to succeed in finally seeing the reality of what you are, thereby redeeming yourself and transforming your life. That is not the point of the inquiry. The point of the inquiry is to look for yourself, to *try* to see reality, just for the sake of seeing what is real, what is true, what is actual. And it is the same with trying to tell the truth in relationships with other people. The best you can do is be resolved to do so.

You are not going to succeed, it is not so easy. You are not going to succeed.

Everything we say, all of our yakking away gets us further from the truth, just like everything we say about the inquiry gets us further from the inquiry, even though it may be necessary to do so. It is the same with telling the truth. Everything we say about any given set of circumstances or relationships moves us further away from the truth of it. It is kind of like marking time, trying to figure out what is to be said. But that is all you can do. And these creatures are not very good at it. We are really not good at telling the truth.

No, I can see that, because I have been struggling with it through the night, and today. And each time you have said something, it has cleared it a little bit further, but this is even better.

Well, that's good.

I see now. And my intent is truly to continue this inquiry.

I am so happy to hear that.

We do get sidetracked in all our activity. But in these few days here, there is such a sense of peace doing it, of quiet, stillness, just looking... Not that you see anything, just the intent of doing it...

Yes, that's right, just looking, because it is the looking that opens up the aperture so the light can shine through, that's all. And the light does the work. The looking does the work of inviting the light, and the light does the work. And that is, of course, a kind of a sweet metaphor, but it's true enough.

It is true enough, absolutely.

And it was very valuable to me to hear, when I was speaking to your husband earlier today, or whenever it was I was speaking to him, and now to you, to see that it really is important to stay in touch, it really is important to stay with it. It really is possible to go back to sleep, because life is so sweet, because it can be so much fun... And then, there you are, and before you know it, you are suffering again, and scared again...

I was thinking about that, too. I have been doing spiritual practice, it seems like forever, but it has probably been thirty years, and I have done hard things, like vipassana sits eleven hours a day, things that were difficult physically and mentally. This is so simple, and so clear, and I was wondering, Why have I fallen back to sleep? Why have I not done this, and allowed myself to become so active? And it's not that I have let it all go, but I...

No, you haven't; obviously, you haven't. It's just momentum.

Is it? Because it was so easy. I don't know...

Partly, it's because it is so easy, but I am not certain of that. Mostly, it is just the momentum of the life, the momentum of this apparatus. Without the continuous bringing into conscious awareness this that is always in awareness, the apparatus generally tends to want to go back to what seems to be easy, and the only reason it is easy is because it is old, it has been running a long time. But even with that, you are still the same. You haven't changed, you haven't been hurt by it, you haven't been diminished by it, you are not enhanced by anything, you are just as you always were. How can it hurt to look at that, as you are climbing the rock wall? You guys don't climb rock walls anymore?

Yes, we do.

What an opportunity.

Yes.

I am glad you are here.

Thank you. I am glad to be here. I would like to continue this for the rest of the week. Thank you.

This has been the best retreat, ever. You guys are magnificent. I will have more to say about all of that tomorrow. I don't have anything else to say now, except to thank you again. I am blown away by your generous willingness to speak with me about these things, to look at yourself, to consider the possibility that life doesn't need to be the way it has been, that life doesn't need to be fraught with fearfulness. Just to consider the possibility of that, despite what must be for all of us here a lengthy history of disappointment with the spiritual endeavor — either a disappointment or a denial of the disappointment.

I am so grateful that you are generous enough to consider the possibility that life doesn't need to be fraught with suffering and misery. And to try this simple, uncomplicated practice of trying to see yourself, trying to apperceive yourself, just to see what happens as a result of it, just to see if there is any truth to it.

So, I am going to go now, and I will be back tomorrow morning. And we will doubtless have an emotional parting. I love you all. Thank you for this time.

Meeting 8

November 6, 2007 - Morning

Well, good morning. Welcome back. You get to go first this morning. With one provision: no expressions of gratitude or expressions of how well you are doing, or how everything is working smoothly. *(laughter)* I know how wonderful you are doing, and I am as flooded with gratitude as you are. Since this is the last day, this is your last chance, this is kind of the last bus out of hell. Let's reserve the seats for those who are still in hell. *(laughter)* So, who has problems? It doesn't exactly have to be problems, but at least questions...

Well, I have been in hell for a little over twenty four hours, hell like I had never experienced before in my life. I am confused about something I think you may have said the other night. I am not a hundred percent clear about what you said, because sometimes I don't hear through my ears, I don't hear words necessarily to learn or grasp, so I may have been confused. I want to clarify it. So, if one inquires about who is seeing, and who is sensing and tasting, etc., and, in that moment, there is an innocent dropping away of the frame of this person, and there is just a pure, crystal-clear consciousness seeing, tasting, and so on, is that a state?

Of course, anything that was not here, and now is here, and then disappears, is a state. It doesn't make it bad. It is not wrong. It is not anything, except a state. Some states are really good. They feel really good; they are in harmony with reality. Some states are really bad. They feel really bad, and they are in disharmony with reality. But their essential nature is the same: they are states of consciousness that appear, and play for a while, and then disappear. The states that are in harmony with reality are kind of a two-edged sword, because on the one hand, they give us the encouragement to continue, and on the other hand, they give us the opportunity to mistake them for reality. So, does that answer your question?

It does. I feel like I'm screwed.

You do? You feel like you're screwed?

I do.

And who would that be? What form does this screwing take?

What do you mean? Could you say that again?

What form does this take?

Being screwed?

Yes.

Like death. It feels like nothing I have ever done ever has meant anything. Nothing means anything.

And what if it doesn't? Why is that such a catastrophe?

I am on the edge of a blade right now, and it is like it could go either way. It is a catastrophe because this individual understands jack shit. And on the other hand, it is like it doesn't matter. And I don't know what to do.

What you do, the only thing you can do, is find out what you are. That is the only thing you can do. You cannot, by any exertion whatsoever, determine the reality or unreality of those things that you have thought and believed, and striven to accomplish or to bring to the world, or what their effect has been. The only thing that is accessible to you is the reality of you. That is the only thing that stays. That is present when the state of crystal-clear consciousness is here, and it is present when the state of impending doom is here. It is the same in both cases. So, the only possibility remaining for you is to move your attention to see directly, for yourself, what you are. That is the purpose of your life. The purpose of your life is not to attain crystal-clear consciousness, or bring joy to the world, or bring misery to the world. The purpose of your life is to see yourself. That is the whole reason we take these forms, the whole reason we spend so much time attending to the state of our thoughts, our emotions and our feelings, our desires and our aversions. It is because we desperately want to see what we are.

And there is never an end to the seeing.

Of course not. There is no end to you. What there is an end to is fear, anxiety, misery, and suffering in the life. All the things that have transpired in your life, they are not what you think they are, but they have brought you to the end of the road. You are right, you are on the edge. You are on the edge, and you have the choice of descending into catastrophe and hellishness, or looking at yourself. Face up to it. You are fearless. Face up to it. See what you are.

Thank you.

You are very welcome. Will you keep in touch with me?

Yes.

Okay. That is the other side of the discovery of the possibility that the life is beside the point. The other side of that is the projection of meaning on the beside-the-pointedness of life, and the meaning almost always would have to be that "My god, I have been so stupid, and everything I have done is worthless and trash." And, of course, that is just another way of infusing meaning and pointedness to the life. But what are you? Maybe the life is absurd, pointless; maybe the life has been wasted, tossed away. Maybe everything you think has been stupid, but what are you?

Something bizarre happened to me last night, and I wanted to ask you about it, but first I need to tell you what led up to it. Yesterday, after the morning meeting, I went back to my room, and I thought, "Well, this is the day before the end of the retreat, and I just don't get it, so I just gotta buckle down and just really work on this." So I sat down in a chair, and I started trying to look at myself. And then after a while, I tried to look at myself while I was standing up, and then while I was walking around, and then while I was looking at nature. Then I just became so exhausted and I finally lay down for about thirty minutes, and then it was time to come to the evening meeting. So, after the evening meeting, I went back to my room, and I was feeling kind of depressed, I think I suffer from chronic depression anyway, but I was thinking, "I'm still not getting this." Intellectually, when you talk, or when other people talk, I can kind of understand, I try to grasp it that way, but I realize, after that experience, that I can't get it that way, that you just can't get it with the intellect. So I thought, "Well, okay, maybe if I write about it, maybe that will help." So I sat down and I started to write, and I wrote, "What is wrong with me? I don't get this." And I started crying, like now, and then suddenly I went

numb. So I wrote that, too. I wrote. "And now I'm numb." And within about less than a minute after writing that, I started to sob. And I lay down on the bed, and I am just sobbing, and I just let it go. After a while, I suddenly realized that there was someone else watching me sob. There was something or someone else watching me sob. I continued to sob, but I thought, "What is that?" And it didn't seem like it was me. But there was no one else in the room, so who else could it be? (laughter) It was just very bizarre. Then, finally, I finished sobbing, and went about my business. My question is, What in the hell was that?

Well, it was you, of course. What else could it be? Nobody else in the room, right? I don't know if you have heard it, but I have spoken a couple times at this retreat about the possibility, maybe even the probability, that one who is trapped in the belief that I am this life and this is all there is to me, may very well perceive the reality of one's nature as some other, apart from oneself. After all, what is happening here is the effort being taken within the conscious personality to see the reality of its own nature. And it is to be expected. You are not alone in this. The idea of god was created in human mind by the perception of a greater being watching the lesser being. But that is you.

I thought I was going nuts.

Well, that's okay, you can go nuts, but that is you. And that's all. What else could it be? Maybe you are going nuts, but still, it is you. I wouldn't rule out being nuts, but that is still you. *(laughter)*

Thanks, John. Yesterday I think I heard you say something about using the word "listening". Did you mean it as in "listening to yourself"?

Every time I say something to you about what it is you are looking for, I am taking you a step back from what you are looking for, into that word or that metaphor. So, if I say to you, look for yourself, or see yourself, that is not really what I am asking you to do. It is a step back from that. It is a substitute for what I am really asking you to do which, once you start trying to do it, will become clear to you. I have in the past said, instead of "look at yourself", "listen to yourself", because listening has a different flavor to it, a more passive flavor, perhaps, than looking. And the actual reality of receiving the certainty of reality is very passive. Although you may very actively struggle and work as you did last night, trying to accomplish the meeting with yourself, in the actual meeting itself, this personality is totally passive. It is absolutely just receiving. So, that is why I sometimes use the word "listening" rather than "looking", just to switch things up, to keep you from thinking that what I am saying has any real meaning; that what I am saying about what you should be doing really is like seeing, or like listening, or like anything else.

I notice that this entity, or whatever it was that felt like it was apart from myself and was watching me sob, was very subtly, very calmly watching me as I was sobbing. And that felt very passive.

Was it familiar?

I guess so. I don't know.

You keep at it, okay? This is a great stroke of good news, it really is. What you see is you. What you want to do is determine for yourself that that is the case, or that that is not the case. You need to determine for yourself whether this is reality. And you know, when I say, "reality", let me just digress for one moment here, because I have been meaning to say this and I keep forgetting. Will you bear with me, please?

Sure.

When I say, "reality", I don't mean to say that life is unreal. It is not that. I don't mean to say that thoughts are unreal even, or that experience is unreal. When I speak about reality, I am speaking about it in the sense that you are the only *self-existing* reality there is. Everything else in the world: bodies, thoughts, memories, expectations, relationships, what you see, what you hear, everything else in the world is conditioned, which means it arises, and it has its existence only because of its relationship to all the other things in the world. It has no self-sufficient existence to it, and that is what I mean when I say "real" and "unreal". Not "unreal" as in "it is not here". Of course, it is here. You are here. The body is here, sort of, conditionally, contingently.

But you are here without condition. When everything else goes, you remain. When everything else changes, you stay the same. And that is what I mean when I say "reality". So you need to determine for yourself whether this is reality, or some other contingent arising, some other experience that you are concocting. And the way you determine that for yourself is, you keep the practice going, you continue trying to look at yourself, you continue to strive with all your heart to meet yourself face-to-face, nakedly, without understanding. And as these experiences arise, you look for the possibility that they are not new, that they are familiar, that in fact what you are seeing, you have always seen. The only criterion for determining reality from unreality is permanence.

So, if it is something that appears, and is very beautiful, and very peaceful, and very quiet, and very sweet, but it hasn't been here before it appeared, and then it disappears, then it is a state. It doesn't mean it's bad, it doesn't mean even that you are on the wrong track. In fact, if anything, quite the opposite, because this inquiry can have that effect — although not always. I am always surprised when I learn of these instances, but for some, it seems, it is very easy. It is just like, "Oh, right. I see." "Wow, that's a relief!" And on about my business.

But the inquiry, especially for those of us, like me, who are deeply invested in the idea that 'I am this life', the inquiry can stir up huge states, huge experiences, good and bad, corrupt and pure. The inquiry has this side-effect of weakening and crippling the control that we hold over our life and the way that it looks, so that all the stuff that I have tried so desperately to exclude from my picture of myself, those strategies are no longer working the way they did. So, the inquiry can be the cause of great experiences of both kinds: huge depression, huge horror, huge hell, huge grace, huge clarity and peacefulness. And it is your job, with your natural intelligence, and your natural capacity to discern in an adult manner, to determine that. And not in order to say, "Oh, bad, I've got to stop that from happening." But in order to say, "Ah. Okay, so what am I, then? If this isn't what I am looking for, what am I then? Who is seeing this? In what does this appear?" That is where intelligence and discernment come to play, and nobody can help you there. Nobody is going to go with you there and say, "Wait a minute, hold it. Not there."

If I really think about this... First of all, this thing watching this entity, which I guess was me, watching me...

It was you, no matter what.

It didn't scare me, so I don't think it was new. And I remember something similar one time when I was injured, and also I have been through other things, like surgeries... For example, the time when I was being injured and everything slowed down and went really, really in slow-motion as it was happening, and I remember, during that time, I was in pain, but also there was this calmness, this surrender to what was happening. And it is kind of like that.

It sounds like you to me. Keep up the work, keep up the inquiry, and it will be clear to you. It will be. The last time we spoke in Santa Monica, we talked about the depression and the fact that when the depression is here, you are here, you are not different. So just continue the inquiry. I am really happy to see you. Look how beautiful you are.

Thank you.

You are welcome. There is a whole school of spiritual instruction that has to do with witness consciousness — which itself is a state. It is a state that can be conjured up, and that has a lot in common with reality, but it is of course a state. And the appearance of witness consciousness is an invitation to find out to whom it appeared. And I am not saying that is what your experience was, because I really don't think it was, but all these things happen. All these things that are reported in the spiritual writings, these are all things that happen. They are just not what we think they are; they are just not what we make of them. Okay, who else? You are next, back in the back, you were first.

When everything is stripped so naked, it is hard to find any place to question anything. Yesterday you mentioned to someone, if it is part of your nature to be coldhearted and you discover that, that is just the way it is. What about if I discover that I am fearful in my nature, and that is just the way it is? How does one change that? Because the nature of what we are doesn't change.

Let me clarify something. I don't know who I was speaking to, or what the context was, but I was speaking about the fact that if you are a coldhearted person, you are going to be just a coldhearted person, and maybe it will change, and maybe it won't change, but that is not you. That is not what I refer to as "you". You know, context is everything, and since we have so few pronouns, I use the same pronoun when I am speaking about the life, as I do when I am speaking about reality. It is possible to get into this excruciating effort to twist oneself into a language style that in some way conforms to the idea of non-dual reality, but I don't have time for that, that is just too exhausting... So I just say "you". And if I am talking about your life, and the way your life is unfolding, I may very well say, "Well, that might just be the nature of you." But I don't mean *you*...

No, I understand that. I am talking about me, discovering inside myself...

Reality.

My reality.

You have no qualities.

Those are all just layers...

That's right, that is all part of your life. You have no qualities like that.

I understand that.

We ascribe qualities to you, because it is just what we do. But we always do so with such trepidation. You are 'silent', for example. It sounds like it is a quality, but it really isn't. And you are 'permanent', for example. That sounds like a quality, too, but it really isn't. It is just a clue; it is just a hint, a direction. But you have no qualities of fearfulness, or coldness, or warmth. You just are what you are. Like Popeye. *(laughter)*

Well, thanks, John. I'll just go and eat more spinach. *(laughter)*

Okay. Was that helpful?

That's great. Thank you.

Okay.

☙

Hi, John. Ever since we talked last night, I just have so many tears coming... And I am feeling like, I don't know, I am just back to square one or something...

Well, you are back to square one. That is where you start, that is where you end. When you are back to square one now, it is a wonderfully good sign. The heartache, the brokenheartedness that you are feeling is a mourning for what you imagine to be the wrong turnings of your life. It is a mourning for what you imagine to be your stupidity prior to this. But that is all imagination, this life lives itself perfectly. There is absolutely nothing you have to say about the way this life unfolds, and it is great good luck that you find yourself back at square one. It's not bad, it's good; it's not a bug, it's a feature. And you can expect that there may very well be a huge arising of remorse, and mourning, and grieving, like, "I have wasted it all, I have just wasted the whole thing." But it is just not true. And even if it is true, what to do? What to do? You are here, now.

I guess that's also that what I mistook for here/now is a state. We talked about the bliss, the silence, the seeing the 'me' as unreal, and then it coming back. So, if that was just an experience, to me it was kind of a hope that this is it, maybe.

Do you see how the automatic apparatus of judgment comes into play? "If that was just an experience…" It is not "just" an experience, it is an experience. It is not "just" a state, it is a state. And it is a gift. It is not a curse, it is a gift.

And that was the other thing I was seeing, how this mind will take something that is a gift…

… and turn it into a curse.

Right.

That's right. But what is that to you? Have you been hurt by it? Look and see. Have you been affected? Touched? Diminished by it? Look and see. What are you? That is the inquiry, and that is the way the vicissitudes and the horror stories of life and the stupidity of the mind become your allies, because all of that is occurring *within* you. The one thing that is the same now as it was when the state of grace was present, exactly the same, is you.

So when you say "Look at yourself", in the seeing, in that state of grace, if we can call it that, if I see that as myself, but I don't see that at another time, then perhaps what you are saying is that this is the work, even when that isn't there? Because when I look at myself, I feel that I am not seeing what I am looking at…

Of course you are not seeing that, that is a state. It is not here anymore. You are here. And there are other states that are now present, like a state of maybe remorse, or regret, or whatever. That is not you, either; it is no more you than the state of grace was. But what this brings to light is just exactly that, that this state that I am feeling now cannot be me. It can't be. It is not here all the time, and I am. The state of grace is not here all the time, and I am. Once the focus of your attention shifts to the discovery of the reality of what you are, then all things whatsoever help, not hinder. They help, because the one thing that is true about you, that is true about nothing else, is that *you are always here.*

The purpose of the inquiry, the purpose of the work is not to produce in you a new state of grace, although states of grace will still come, I guarantee you. You are not done with them. The purpose of the work is not to create in you a new state of grace, or to make permanent what is, by its nature, temporary, but to rid you of the idea that you are the one who is subject to all this, subject to passing states of grace, and passing states of hell. That is the purpose of the inquiry.

And as we enter into the spiritual arena, into the spiritual work, it is just natural to think that. What else are we going to think, except that what we are after is that state of grace made permanent? How could I think anything other than that, until I come face-to-face with the fact that the only thing I can know, and the only thing I can have, and the only thing I can be certain of is *me?* Then we begin to see, and this natural capacity for discernment begins to make itself known. We begin to be able to see, not: "Oh, my god, the state of grace was a lie, it was false, it was the devil's work." But simply, "Ah!" Just "Ah!"

Then I am not really sure that I know what self-inquiry is.

That is a very good place to be. I will tell you, but I can't do it for you. Self-inquiry is the effort to come face-to-face with the actual reality of what you are, with your actual nature — and know it to be so. That's what self-inquiry is. It requires you to bring to bear your natural intelligence, your common sense, your capacity for discernment, and to try. And try some more. And you won't do it right. But I promise you from my heart, if you try, you will succeed. This effort cannot be denied; it has never been denied to anyone. If you make the effort, if you make it your purpose to be certain of what you are once-and-for-all, you cannot be denied.

And I know that no one can give me that.

That's right. I can help, right? I can help you. I can say, "No, not that," but I can't give it to you. And I can't predict what course it will take in you.

Well, this was a surprise. This was a surprise.

This was a good surprise. Yes, this is a good surprise, believe me. *(laughter)*

Right. Thank you.

You are very welcome.

⌒

I am very happy to see your hand up this morning.

I just wanted to continue the conversation that we had last night. I mentioned that I stopped being a seeker for a few years, after seeing that I was not the doer. I was clear. When I mentioned that the seeker appeared again, you asked me, "Why did it appear?" And it seemed to me that I couldn't answer that question, but now it is very simple. Regarding my health, the issues that I have had, the seeking for health brought back the seeker altogether, on all levels. It just brought the seeker back, that's all. I don't want this in my life, I want to be better, I am not accepting this, which is truly different than before. So, that is the answer.

Well, that's good, I am happy to hear that. That is a reasonable, rational explanation for that. If the seeker came back, the seeker was never gone. But we don't really have to talk about that. We don't have to talk about the time when the seeker wasn't here, and when you weren't the doer, and all that. That is in the past now. Whatever has caused it to be in the past, it is in the past. What I have to tell you, and what I have to offer you, no matter that there was a time in your life when you thought all this was over, is that what you are seeking, what you are really seeking, the only thing that will satisfy you is the face-to-face meeting with the reality of what you are. That is all that will satisfy you. You may be able to go away from it again, but in the end, that is all that will bring it to an end.

And the proof of that is that the misery came with the experience of the non-health, and the health issues. And all the grief that went with that, because of the loss of the physical activities I used to do.

Because that was so big a part of your definition of yourself.

It was just to be in the world, like other people are.

Yes, right. And I am not saying that your aspiration was exceptional, but it was nevertheless, as it is with everybody, a huge part of your definition of what you are.

Absolutely.

And now that has been brought into question, or destroyed, or otherwise shaken...

Yes. But the proof that there was something that was not finished is that I was identified with the person who was not healthy.

Yes. That's what I am saying. So, here you are, just as you have always been. The only thing you can do is look at yourself.

Okay, John, at this point, I have done this for ten months.

And what is your result?

Like I have said, I am a very good practitioner, and I have done it every single day, and for about fifteen to twenty times a day.

And what have you done?

What have I done? I sat with myself, and I closed my eyes, and I looked... And I sat with the sense of presence that I felt. Sometimes, in the morning I would do that, and sometimes it was more like flashes of "Am I conscious that I am here? Yes, I am." And I just got in touch with the sense of something that would be more like the air that feels like me.

Okay.

It's very much like nothing. So I did that for the past ten months. Last night, I still had a lot of grief about that, about the loss of my energy level, my health, and that is also proof that this hasn't worked at all.

Grief is a proof of that?

Yes, because I am identified with the person who is not healthy.

I am not disputing you, but what is your evidence that you are identified with this person? Just because you say so?

The big grief that I feel.

Grief comes and goes.

And a non-acceptance of it, and the wanting it to be over.

Why is that a problem?

Because it creates misery.

For whom?

For me.

For the air that feels like you?

No, not for that.

Well, then it doesn't create misery for you. Listen to me. It takes time. There is a long-standing habit of identification, and there is a long-standing habit of thinking, "I'm still identified." So what? You know what you are, right? You are the air that feels like you. Why do you care about the grief and the sense of identification with the person? I mean this literally, I am not trying to trick you. Why is that a problem? What makes that a problem?

Something in me tells me that if I had a clear, deep seeing of what I am, and if I were established truly in what I am...

This is spiritual talk. You have a really clear seeing of what you are. You have never been missing a clear seeing of what you are. The only thing that has been in operation, and continues to be in operation to a lesser extent, is the belief that you are this life. The belief that you are this life alone is what produces the perception that grief or misidentification are the problem.

Okay, then I believe that I am the life. That is the proof that it is not working.

Well, it hasn't worked yet, entirely. It takes time. Do you know how long it took me? It took me two years before I even realized that "You know what? Actually, that works." Right up until the last moment, I was saying, "This doesn't work." Now, I tell you that it does work, and it is working in you. There is a strong inclination to pay a lot of attention to the fact that it feels like a problem.

When I am in a context like this, in a spiritual retreat, yes.

If it is not like that when you are not in a spiritual retreat, then you must be kind of zoning out. Why would it be different here than there?

It is a little bit less intense... No, I am not zoning out.

I am glad to hear that. Okay, so here's the deal, here is the actual fact of the matter. You really do know how to do the inquiry. You really do have a sense of the reality of what you are. You really are able to expose your life and your personal consciousness to the reality of what you are, and still, there is the sense of a problem because of the grief. The grief seems to cause problems, and it seems it should not be here.

I still think that I am my life.

Right, because there remains some vestige of the belief that you are your life. Or at least you think there does. But so what? Keep it up. It is really important to see this. The truth is that this is not like, Bam! Everything is right, everything is clean, everything is clear. We are dealing with a very powerful practice that is affecting an extraordinarily strong, deep-seated, continuously-fed and encouraged habit of belief. It takes time.

Okay, one other question. When you said that if you take yourself to be your life, then you have all this fear and this anxiety... Can you illustrate that in some way, for example, when I go to the store, or I go to take a plane, what does that feel like?

I don't have a whole lot of memory of it, but my recollection of it goes like this. You go through life, and there is this undercurrent that is not always big, and is not always even noticeable. But there is an energetic undercurrent of being careful that you don't do the wrong thing, think the wrong thing, want the wrong thing, try to get rid of the wrong thing. And, for the most part, this is like a murmur of at-stakeness. That is the anxiety I speak of. At times, it flares up into a fire of fearfulness, "Oh, my god, I have done something wrong. I have failed. Oh, wait a minute, I wish I could take that back." Or, "Oh, my god, I'm gonna die." Now, here is the big one: "Oh, my god, I'm gonna die." And the fear of death is so huge that it really kind of resists even seeing, or touching, or having anything to do with, because it is taboo. That is the hugest example of the fearfulness I speak of.

That anxiety and fearfulness is what characterizes the life of one who believes oneself to be at stake in the life, one who believes oneself to be the life. And that is always present. I mean, not when you are in deep sleep, and not when you take antidepressants, but other than that, it is always present. As long as you are alive, and awake, and moving around in the world, and even sometimes when you are asleep, it is there. This is what the Buddhists call *dukkha*, the off-centeredness, this kind of unsatisfactoriness. *Dukkha* is a Pali word, and it refers to a wheel, the axis of which is slightly off-center. So that, no matter how good things are going, no matter how bad things are going, there is still this little: "Not quite right. Not quite right. What is it? What is going on? What can I do?" That is what I am speaking of. And that comes to an end. But it takes time. And I will tell you something else, too. It is my experience that the belief, and the attendant misery and suffering, actually, for me, were gone long before I knew they were gone. They were gone, and I continued maintaining that they were not gone.

Thank you.

These apparatuses have their own life, almost. They have come into being, contingent and conditioned on all the circumstances in which they appear. They shift and change — they change their direction, they change what they look like, what they are moving toward, what they are moving against, what they are accepting, what they are rejecting — in accordance with changing circumstance and the way things are, and this has been going on forever. So it continues going on for a while. Papaji used to talk about the ceiling fan. You have a ceiling fan that is running, and running, and running. You turn off the electricity, and the ceiling fan still keeps running, and running, and running… *(laughter)* Until it stops. It is like that.

But keep up the inquiry, because your description is authentic. I was taken by surprise. This business of "It's like the air that feels like me", that is very evocative of what I am talking about. It is not true, but… *(laughter)* So, it is quite possible that it is really over, and you just don't know it. It is like a phantom limb, right? So just stick with it. It seems sometimes like a huge trick that they have played on us by pulling us into this business with all these promises of enlightenment, and transcendence, and levitation, and all that stuff, and now we are stuck with just doing the work, and waiting for the consequences; taking the action, and waiting for the karmic unfolding. This is the action, this is the karma that ends karma, that's what this is. But it takes time for its effects to be felt. And its effects are, however, well worth waiting for. I mean, you have been waiting for them all your life.

We have been doing these retreats in the fall for five years now. And until now, it seems to me that maybe every time before this one, our feeling was, "Okay, this is the last one, this is it." And we don't see anything that could create the circumstances whereby a retreat like this could happen again. And, of course, every time we have thought that, no matter how many times that has been, we have turned out to be wrong. And here we are again, at the end of a fall retreat here in Ojai. A retreat the like of which we have never seen before. But of course, that is true every time, too. *(laughter)* And I can't conceive of a set of circumstances that would prevent us from doing this again.

These gatherings together in retreat toward the end of the year have been for us an opportunity to reflect on the state of the discourse in this business of self-inquiry. Since we don't have the claim or the interest in infallibility and enlightened transmission that can make you think that there is nothing to be learned, or nothing to be changed in the state of the discourse that is of any interest, we are stuck with trying to do this work as well as we can, trying to be as effective and useful as we can to the people who come to us. Trying to make use of the reports that we hear, and the problems that are reported, and the successes that are reported, to hone our expression, and to refine it, and to make it more useful for the future. During the year, we are out there and we are speaking to people. Many things come to me during these meetings with you, whatever form you take, wherever you are. Many things, many understandings come to me about how to offer this possibility, how to be helpful and not a hindrance to the natural efforts of people everywhere to be happy.

I think that my expression in this has changed. It is really interesting to me, and this is my report to you. It is a report on the state of the discourse. It is interesting to me that I have recently just had the opportunity in passing to hear something I was talking about a long time ago. I don't remember whether it was a recording or a videotape, and I was astonished to see that, actually, I have been saying the same thing for as long as I have been speaking, although it seems to me that I am saying it differently now than I was then. It seems to me that I have become more skilled at speaking about this over the years, but it is shocking and actually kind of confirming to see that I was always saying the same thing.

This year is the first year that we have completely eliminated fees and suggested donations from our meetings with people. We did that because it came to me very clearly that I want to talk to everybody, and that means I want to talk to those who can, and will, pay for a meeting. I want to talk to them. But I want to also talk to those who cannot, or even will not, pay. I want to talk to everybody. And when I saw that, it was very apparent to me that the only solution to that was to just completely abandon all transactional relationship in this work. And if the work has value, then support will come. And so far, that has been true.

But the amazing thing about the change, and this is the first retreat that has been done under that policy, is how confirmed we are in the value of doing what we are doing. We have gathered together here the largest retreat we have ever had. I am sure there are people among us here who would be unable to pay a fee, there are people here who would be able to pay a fee, and there are people who have come who would not have come if there was money attached to it, even though they could have paid. And the mix of the people in this retreat is a miracle.

I am sorry about talking about money, but it is what we do, right? In the past, when we charged for retreats, we mostly got people who have been with us for a while, people who have paid in the past, and would continue to pay in the present, who have had a history and a long-term relationship with us. This time, we have a retreat that is amazing in the attendance. It is just amazing. We actually have people who never were in a meeting with me before. And we have people who have been with us for a long time. And we have people who have been with us off and on, and so forth. We have people who already had a really good understanding of what it is we are trying to offer, and we have people who had no idea what we are trying to offer. And what a difference to me this has made. How valuable this has been to me, to my ability to do this work, which is to bring the possibility that is present in the practice of self-inquiry to everybody I can get ahold of. How much it has enriched my own understanding of the way this teaching can be expressed. It has been unbelievable. I am floored in gratitude for the presence of everybody here, for the participation, the enthusiastic and heartfelt participation of everybody in this retreat. This has been the best retreat ever.

In the ultimate sense, it really doesn't matter what happens to humanity. In ultimate reality, it really doesn't matter if humanity is wiped out of the universe tomorrow. The universe, reality, you, would be unaffected by it. Nothing is touched or hurt or harmed or helped by humanity's glory or humanity's horror. Nothing. Humanity itself is a passing fancy; it arose out of who knows what circumstances. A passing fancy, of no more consequence than the dodo, which of course is now long gone, and nobody notices its absence.

But, from within a human life, it seems much different. It is very difficult, from within a human life, to convincingly make the claim that humanity is unimportant and insignificant. Within a human life, especially within a human life that has been, as all of ours have been to one degree or another, if you will forgive the expression, "enlightened", a life that has been touched by the light of reality, it is very difficult not to lament the possibility of the passing of humanity. We are amazing. This capacity for self-consciousness, this capacity for the self-reflective entertaining of what reality is, seems to be, so far as we can tell, unique to human beings. The arising even of the thought, "What am I?" The arising even of the thoughts, "What is this? Why is it? From whence does it come? To where does it return? What is going on here?"

I hate to sink into metaphysics, but it seems to me that the entire cosmos, the entire world, everything that exists, the capacity for existence itself is an outcome of the impossibility of awareness (which is all there is) to *be* without an object, to *be* without seeing itself. Papaji always said that the self is endlessly in love with seeing itself. And although that language is a little strange to my ears, it certainly is the truth. Reality certainly is in love with seeing itself. And it is that single aspect of reality, the only quality of reality there is, that gives rise to this whole cosmos, all of it. And here, in human beings, awareness has the potential and the possibility of consciously seeing itself, of being conscious of the reality of it, of seeing itself as you and me, as hatred and love, as horror, as hell, as heaven, as light and darkness. And that is hard to see as being insignificant and irrelevant from within a human life.

And, of course, all of us, we see what we see from within a human life. That is the gift of a human life. This stone floor has, as its essential nature, the same essential nature as you and I have, but the stone floor doesn't seem to have the capacity of self-reflection, of being able to know what it sees — and we do. That is amazing. That is incomprehensible. It is impossible to come up with a theoretical basis that explains why that should have come about, and why in us, in these bodies.

And now, it seems that humanity is hell-bent, and absolutely determined to wipe itself out. It really does. Look at the news. Look at what is going on in the world. In its essential nature, it is no different from what has been going on for all of human history, since the time we crawled out of the caves and began stabbing each other with sharpened bones, and beating each other with sticks and stones. But it is the magnitude of it. We have such power, we have gotten much, much better at murder than we were in the beginning. And we got so good at murder that we do it unconsciously by turning the planet against us, the planet which now seems itself to be trying to get rid of us.

So it is quite possible that humanity doesn't have much time left and that this amazing, incomprehensible arising of self-reflective consciousness in human beings is doomed and will go quickly. It is possible that the whole of humanity will be, as you have been reporting about your life, just a waste of time. It is possible that it will turn out to be a waste of time, that we just pissed it away. And part of how we piss it away is by turning the energy that arises within us to find the truth and to see what is real into the worship of gods and goddesses, of heaven and hell, of celebrity and wealth, and pleasure. God, I am beginning to sound like an Old Testament prophet! *(laughter)*

But really, it is the case. And it is the perception of this that makes the promulgation of this teaching so vital. Not vital in the sense that anything is going to be harmed if we do get wiped off, but vital in the sense of seeing what we can do; of seeing, finally, what it is possible for humanity to do with this incredible, unbelievable, incomprehensible gift of self-reflection, of self-consciousness, this gift of the ability to suffer, to want to be this, to want to be the other thing, the gift of the yearning for truth, the yearning for an end to stupidity.

And it is my experience, and the experience of many that I have been with over this time, that for the individual human being, this is the only possibility for bringing an end to the misery. The misery doesn't really have to be huge; it doesn't have to be like hell. Hell is actually kind of a welcome break from the monotony of the continuous, underlying murmuring anxiety and fearfulness of feeling that you are at stake in this life.

But this practice, which I am certainly not infallible in passing on, is this possibility that exists within us as human beings — and, so far as we know, nowhere else in the entire universe — of actually perceiving reality directly; no matter how gross and limited our senses and our sensibilities are, we actually have this capacity to perceive reality directly. And the perception of reality, directly, without understanding, actually does destroy the belief that we are these lives. It actually does. It takes time, it is not the same for everybody, but in the end, that belief goes, when exposed to the light of reality. And just as that is the only hope for the individual human being, it is the only hope for humanity, too.

Really, there is nothing else. We have tried everything else. We have tried every political solution. We have tried slavery, we have tried feudalism. We have tried murder. We have tried capitalism, we have tried democracy, we have tried fascism, we have tried Nazism, we have tried communism. None of them work. Otherwise, we wouldn't be in this mess today, right? If one of them had worked, we would be done with it.

We have tried every kind of therapeutic solution that we can come across: psychotherapy, drugs, electrotherapy, water therapy, everything. The list is even longer than the political efforts we have tried. *(laughter)* And they haven't worked, either. They can be useful, they can be helpful, in certain cases, at certain times, but they haven't worked. The test of having worked is that we wouldn't be in this mess. We have tried enlightenment, we have tried mantras, we have tried chanting, we have tried japa, and we have tried accepting Jesus as our savior. We have tried hydrogen bombs, going to the Moon, literature, music, art. We have tried it all, and still, here we are, every day closer to the destruction of humanity.

So, when we come to the spiritual realm, we come with blinders on. "Okay, I want to get better, I want to be enlightened, I want to be rid of this, I want my life to be like the Buddha's life. Give it to me, give it to me." And we work, and we meditate, and we chant, and we do mantras, and we get big states, and little states, we get hell realms and heaven realms, and jealous god realms, all of that. Still here, same old, same old. The Tibetans get kicked out of Tibet by the Chinese, murdered, slaughtered. Here we are, still the same.

This practical, non-spiritual practice is not in the realm of spirituality, this is in the realm of reality, of the determination to know reality. Not the determination to be enlightened, or to be at peace, or to be happy, or to experience 360-degree consciousness, but the realm of the determination to know reality. This practice has proven itself to me, to my satisfaction, in my own life and in the life of a lot of people who have been with me over these last eight years. This practice, in the realm of the determination to see what is real, actually works, and it actually rids the individual human being of the belief that they are at stake in this life. It actually rids the individual human life of the undercurrent, the murmuring anxiety and the fires of fearfulness that plague us all. And as it does that, it actually rids the individual human life of the internal warfare that is the source of all warfare whatsoever, the internal warfare that says, "I have to have this" and "I have to get rid of that." All warfare arises from that two-step dance.

This practice actually does away with that internal antagonism that says, "This thought is going to send me to hell. Go away." And "This feeling is going to make me happy. Come here, don't leave. Don't go. I'll kill you if you go."

In the realm of the determination to see reality, so far as I can tell, from all of the history of humanity, this practice holds out the only hope that humanity can survive its own murderous intent, because if it wipes out this internal warfare in me and in you, it wipes out the internal warfare in all. And it wipes out all of the energy that makes George Bush know that *he* is right, and that the world must conform to *his* view of things, in order for there to be peace and happiness in the world, or Musharraf's view of that. I used to be a Communist revolutionary, because I wanted to save the world. That didn't turn out too well. And now I seem to be an evangelical, fundamentalist preacher of reality.

That's also revolutionary.

It is much more revolutionary than communism, much more. If the FBI could see me now... *(laughter)* And they are welcome here, too. That is what brings me here. What brings me here is an endlessly renewing, rejuvenating love affair with the possibility that we have, as human beings. And having somehow stumbled upon the key to eternal happiness, I can't do anything but try to bring it to you, and try to learn from you how to bring it to you better.

So, I am unbelievably grateful for this time with you in this retreat. I promise you that it will have a good effect on my work, and I promise you that I am available to you all the time. It doesn't mean that I answer all my emails. But if you need me, write to me, say something to me. I will talk to you on the phone; I will talk to you online. I will be available to you as much as I possibly can be. There are only so many hours in a day, and there are about eight billion people I would like to talk to... *(laughter)*

So, keep up the practice, keep it up. See if you can see how it can be better taught, how it can be better presented. Talk to me about it, write to me, help me. Because the truth is, I swear to god, we are all in this together. Really, we are. We are in the same boat, and we are going to sink or swim together.

So, thank you, thank you. I am your servant. Really, I am at your service. Thank you for this time. Thank you for your attention. Thank you for your willingness. Thank you for this wondrous retreat.

If you enjoyed this book and would like to order additional copies for yourself and for friends, please check with your local bookstore, favorite online bookseller or place your order directly with the publisher at http://www.riverganga.org.

For more information about John Sherman's work, visit: http://www.riverganga.org and http://www.johnsherman.org.

Feedback to the author may be sent by email directly to johnsherman@riverganga.org

About John Sherman

Like many of us, John spent most of his life believing himself to be trapped in a difficult, bewildering and probably meaningless life. Then, in the fall of 1994, he happened upon the world of spiritual aspiration and attainment, of wondrous tales of enlightenment and delicious insights of non-dual understanding and, not for the first time in his life, found himself head-over-heels in love with an idea and, also not for the first time in his life, he threw himself headlong into seeking its promised fruit. Enlightenment ensued.

For the next year and a half he read everything he could get his hands on concerning the quest for liberation: sutras, shastras, upanishads, teachings, stories about teachers and gurus and rinpoches, poetry, philosophy, metaphysical speculation and scriptures from every tradition and religion. He gorged on these beautiful ideas, and got drunk on their promise. He practiced every practice he could find, and fell into samadhi states at will. At the time, he wrote of being able literally to 'hear the stones sing silent arias of Being.'

After about a year of this, his enlightenment collapsed, all the beauty vanished, all sense of clarity and all vestige of spiritual attainment disappeared, and he was left empty-handed, wishing he had never even heard the word *enlightenment* — all the while still caught in the grip of its sweet hope. He has spoken of that time as his 'year in hell.'

He set out to find just *one thing* that he could do for himself that would settle, once and for all, the question whether human life without fear and misery was even possible.

John settled on the teaching of Ramana Maharshi — a teaching that he had once considered "too simple" for his advanced understanding — as the cleanest, most direct, and most likely to lead to the actual truth of the matter. This teaching is sometimes called self-inquiry.

He began reading books with Ramana's conversations with people. He wrestled with Ramana's words, trying to hear with his own inner ear what Ramana was actually suggesting that we *do*. John was looking for a practical course of action that would either work and rid him of his hatred of life, or fail and rid him of the false hope of spiritual deliverance.

He took Ramana's instructions literally. He was done with seeking the fruits of action; now he sought only to find the right action itself and *do* it. In the end, as Ramana often promised, all came out well.

Turns out that it works, this simple effort to get the feel of yourself, this self-inquiry. Not as a spiritual practice (Self-Inquiry), but as an honest effort to get for yourself just the briefest, most fleeting glimpse of *what it actually feels like to be you* — not *I Am*, or *Self,* or *True Self,* or *Beingness,* or *Awareness,* or any such thing. Just you, plain and simple, never-absent, seldom-noticed you… nothing more and nothing less than just you.

John has been trying for more than ten years now to find a way to speak clearly of what he discovered during that year of desperate struggle to escape from the misery of his life. It has become clear to him that we suffer from nothing more than a simple *mistake* as to our actual nature, and that the vocabulary, context and thought forms that make up traditional spiritual discourse are of no real help to us in this matter.

Over the years, as a result of meeting with people, listening to them, engaging with them and learning from them, John has acquired a clear and coherent understanding of the actual problem that afflicts human beings, and he has developed a simple and revolutionary method that brings an end to it; a method so simple that it requires neither understanding nor abandonment of understanding, neither belief nor abandonment of belief; a method that requires nothing at all beyond the willingness to look and notice yourself from time to time, whenever it occurs to you to do so.

John holds annual retreats in Ojai, California. Every year, people from all over the world come to join or rejoin this evolving conversation.

∞

RiverGanga Foundation is a not-for-profit, 509(a)(2) public charitable organization under Section 501(c)(3) of the United States Internal Revenue Code.

Our Internal Revenue Service Employer ID Number is 77-0561647. All donations are tax deductible for US residents as charitable contributions.

For more information on how you can help support our work, visit http://www.riverganga.org/go/support

Index

C

D

U

unconditional 144
understanding 1, 2, 5, 6, 7, 8, 22, 26, 32, 37, 44, 62, 63, 64, 75, 96, 98, 99, 121, 146, 179, 195, 198
unreal 168, 179, 184
unsatisfactoriness 192

V

vasanas 128
vichara 22, 23
vigilant 11, 54

W

war 9, 11
Who am I? 62
wildness 155
willing 9, 13, 21, 56, 138
willingness 1, 11, 13, 14, 171, 200
will-o'-the-wisp 80
witness 2, 75, 181
witnessing 75

Y

yearning 70, 106, 136, 197

Breinigsville, PA USA
17 February 2011
255800BV00002B/6/P